MW00527455

What People Are Saying about
Healing from Incest

Brave, profound, touching, healing. This well-written honest book takes the reader inside the complexities of the therapeutic healing process from the patient and therapist's unique perspective. It is the story of hard work, hope, commitment and recovery!

Susan J. Lewis Ph.D. J.D.

The book before your eyes tells a tale few have the courage to discuss—trauma survivor or counselor. The story of healing and the process of facilitating that healing are discussed in vivid detail. This book calls to all involved in these horrific experiences and helpers alike. *Healing From Incest: Intimate Conversations with My Therapist* is a must read. It shines a light not only into the shadows these acts take place in but also onto the path away from them.

Douglas R. Tillman, PhD, LPC, NCC

In this book, *Healing from Incest*, Geri Henderson and Seanne Emerton have given the reader a window into the life of one who has experienced incest. Her story demonstrates the decades of therapeutic services needed for recovery. Geri's candid dialogue with her therapist of how these experiences of abuse affected her at nearly every turn in life and Seanne's highly skilled interventions and interpretations allow readers to feel as though they are participating in the therapeutic process.

This book goes beyond being of benefit to therapists and victims of abuse. The depth of awareness one walks away with after reading this book can impact how social work is done, inform the juvenile justice system, alter policies of Departments of Health and Human Services as well as change state legislation regulating services to families facing these issues. This book can also give hope to communities that have not been able to escape the cycle of family secrets and abuse. Geri and Seanne show us how one can emerge from years of suffering and be able to successfully navigate their own happiness.

Suzy Schulz, MME
Retired Youth Detention Educator
ODR approved mediator affiliated with
The Mediation Center, Lincoln, Nebraska

Every person who experiences trauma is eventually faced with a choice: to remain a victim of circumstance or fight to become a survivor. With raw honesty, Ms. Henderson tells of the complicated and often devastating effects of incest and of her brave transformation from victim to survivor. Complete with commentary from the therapist that walked the healing journey with Ms. Henderson, *Healing from Incest: Intimate Conversations with My Therapist* will serve as a ray of hope for any incest victim and as a guide for anyone wishing to help them become a survivor.

Sonya Buskirk, M.S., LMHP, CPC

Healing from Incest
Intimate Conversations with My Therapist

Geri Henderson, Ph.D.
&
Seanne Emerton, LMFT, LIMHP, LPC

Biography & Autobiography : Personal Memoirs
Psychology : Psychotherapy - Child & Adolescent
Self-Help : Abuse - General

For information, contact
MSI Press
1760-F Airline Highway, #203
Hollister, CA 95023

Cover photo by Hal Maggiore

Cover design by CDL Services

Library of Congress Control Number 2014948862

ISBN: 978-1-933455-53-2

About the front cover:

kintsukuroi
(n.) (v. phr.) "to repair with gold"; the art of repairing pottery with gold or silver lacquer and understanding that the piece is more beautiful for having been broken.

Acknowledgements

Writing this book was never going to be easy. Chapters were written and discarded many years ago. When I was convinced that the inspiration for the book and this format was my most important mission to date, I knew it would never see the light of day without Seanne's willingness to listen, to believe, and to trust me. I will be forever grateful to her for allowing this book to be written.

Because the book took so long from its inception to its completion, there are many along the way to thank who encouraged, read, and listened. One of our most attentive readers, Sonya Buskirk, was detailed in her criticisms and suggestions. I am so grateful for her help in taking this project seriously and thoughtfully.

There were other readers, friends, and colleagues too who gave us feedback and especially their conviction that this was an important addition to the literature on the topic. Most of all, they said it would be helpful. I am particularly grateful to Gary, Toni, Rich, Sandy, CharlAnn, Jeanette, Eric, Pam, Cynthia, Madeline, Stephanie, Kathryn, Cheryl, and Marty who have been unflagging in their support, not to mention their desire to see its final completion. Some of these individuals were readers; all of them encouraged me to persevere in this rather long process even though the difficulties seemed insurmountable at times. Of special mention is Shari, who provided the concept for the cover and helped me deal with concerns I had about my family.

I was not surprised that my family had reservations about the publication of this book. I have appreciated their thoughtful consideration of the possible implications of such a book and yet their trust in my care to protect them. I love them for allowing me to tell this story, and I hope I have honored their trust.

Although I never really wanted to write this book, I can now say that despite the difficulties in its germination process, I am incredibly grateful for Geri's inner knowing that it needed to be written. Her choice and consent, as well as her family's, to release her personal information for the purpose of this book, and her courage, openness, and honesty in telling her story is not only inspiring but motivating. The writing has been an intense personal and professional journey for which I am forever grateful. I thank Susan Lewis, Ph.D., J.D. for helping me see and embrace the greater good in the telling of this story using our real names. I also thank Theresia and Heike for helping me see this more clearly. I would not have begun this endeavor without the support of my husband, Tom, who has given invaluable insight and feedback. Our children, Nate, Britt, Andrew, and Megan have been supportive in ways that have been especially helpful. I thank my colleagues and friends who have been steadfast in support and feedback: Joni, Pam, Marvin, Shari, Doug, Carlene, Linda, Loyie, Denise and my Family Resources family. Thank you to the many artists who willingly gave their art, time, energy, and inspiration for the cover: Mikey Amedeo, CharlAnn Mitchell, Nancy Fairbanks, and Hal Maggiore. My appreciation also goes to Dr. Howard Tyas for his helpful consultation. Thank you to Jamshed Morenas, my family therapy trainer through Philadelphia Child Guidance Center, who was masterful in teaching the subtle art of doing therapy and the value, power, and complexity of family systems.

Douglas Tillman?

Dedication

We dedicate this work to the *spirit of resilience* that allows healing and growth.

Geri Henderson & Seanne Emerton

There is no greater agony
than bearing an untold story inside you.

Maya Angelou

Geri Henderson & Seanne Emerton

Disclaimer

All names and most situations related to Geri and/or her work with Seanne have been changed. In particular, Geri's siblings are representations. Some events are based on fact, and others are typical of families of incest.

Geri Henderson & Seanne Emerton

Child Sexual Abuse Statistics[1]

- The prevalence of child sexual abuse is difficult to determine because it is often not reported; experts agree that the incidence is far greater than what is reported to authorities. Child sex abuse (CSA) is also not uniformly defined, so statistics may vary. Statistics below represent some of the research done on child sexual abuse.

- The U.S. Department of Health and Human Services' Children's Bureau report *Child Maltreatment* (2010) found that 9.2% of victimized children were sexually assaulted (page 24).

- Studies by David Finkelhor[2], Director of the Crimes Against Children Research Center[3], show that:

  - 1 in 5 girls and 1 in 20 boys is a victim of child sexual abuse;

  - Self-report studies show that 20% of adult females and 5-10% of adult males recall a childhood sexual assault or sexual abuse incident;

  - During a one-year period in the U.S., 16% of youth ages 14 to 17 had been sexually victimized;

---

1   http://www.victimsofcrime.org/media/reporting-on-child-sexual-abuse/child-sexual-abuse-statistics

2   http://www.unh.edu/ccrc/researchers/finkelhor-david.html

3   http://www.unh.edu/ccrc/about/index.html

- Over the course of their lifetime, 28% of U.S. youth ages 14 to 17 had been sexually victimized;

- Children are most vulnerable to CSA between the ages of 7 and 13.

- According to a 2003 National Institute of Justice report[4], 3 out of 4 adolescents who have been sexually assaulted were victimized by someone they knew well (page 5).

- A Bureau of Justice Statistics report[5] shows 1.6 % (sixteen out of one thousand) of children between the ages of 12-17 were victims of rape/sexual assault (page 18).

- A study conducted in 1986 found that 63% of women who had suffered sexual abuse by a family member also reported a rape or attempted rape after the age of 14. Recent studies in 2000, 2002, and 2005 have all concluded similar results (page 8[6]).

- Children who had an experience of rape or attempted rape in their adolescent years were 13.7 times more likely to experience rape or attempted rape in their first year of college (page 9[7]).

- A child who is the victim of prolonged sexual abuse usually develops low self-esteem, a feeling of worthlessness, and an abnormal or distorted view of sex. The child may become withdrawn and mistrustful of adults and can become suicidal (page 1[8])

- Children who do not live with both parents as well as children living in homes marked by parental discord, divorce, or

---

4   https://www.ncjrs.gov/pdffiles1/nij/194972.pdf

5   http://www.bjs.gov/content/pub/pdf/cv10.pdf

6   http://arrow.dit.ie/cgi/viewcontent.cgi?article=1054andcontext=aaschsslartsands ei-redir=1andreferer=http%3A%2F%2Fscholar.google.com%2Fscholar%3Fstart%3 D10%26q%3Dchild%2Bsexual%2Babuse%26hl%3Den%26as_sdt%3D1%2C9%26as_ ylo%3D2009%26as_yhi%3D2012%26as_vis%3D1%26as_s.

7   Ibid, p. 9

8   http://www.aacap.org/iMIS/ContactManagement/Sign_ In.aspx?WebsiteKey=a2785385-0ccf-4047-b76a-64b4094ae07fand

domestic violence have a higher risk of being sexually abused (page 171[9]).

- In the vast majority of cases where there is credible evidence that a child has been penetrated, only between 5% and 15% of those children will have genital injuries consistent with sexual abuse (page 2[10]).

- Child sexual abuse is not solely restricted to physical contact. Such abuse could include noncontact abuse, such as exposure, voyeurism, and child pornography.

- Compared to those with no history of sexual abuse, young males who were sexually abused were five times more likely to cause teen pregnancy, three times more likely to have multiple sexual partners, and two times more likely to have unprotected sex, according to the study published online and in the June print issue of the *Journal of Adolescent Health*[11].

---

9   http://futureofchildren.org/futureofchildren/publications/docs/19_02_FullJournal.pdf

10   http://www.ndaa.org/pdf/GreenUpdateV6N2_NDAA.pdf

11   http://www.jahonline.org/article/S1054-139X(10)00835-9/abstract

Geri Henderson & Seanne Emerton

Contents

1

On the Writing of This Book: An Unusual Collaboration

During the final months of therapy with Seanne, more than ten years ago, I shared the idea of this book with her. Back then, it was just a curious "what if" sort of notion. I thought, "What if someone who could write and who has thought about this recovery process were to collaborate with her therapist on a book?" My initial thought was about how helpful it would have been for me to have had the chance to read such a book. But there was no way to start anything immediately, and it was clear that the idea sounded a bit strange to Seanne though she always expressed support.

After the conclusion of my therapy with her, I moved away and became very involved in my professional career as well as moving on to another therapist. I did revisit the idea of a book from time to time and three or four years later began to write. I approached Seanne again about the possibility of our collaboration. The problem was that other than collaboration, I had no real sense of how this might work. What was obvious was that Seanne did not have the time or a clear sense of how the book would be written. I discovered she was reluctant, considering the past client/therapist relationship, but I was not interested in writing a book without her. I always said I didn't want to write another "poor, miserable me" book that didn't offer any hope of recovery.

I put my writing away and didn't really touch it again for a number of years. About three years ago I returned to it when, after speaking with Seanne, I saw that she was more comfortable with the idea, primarily because more time had passed and she felt we were better positioned to manage this new kind of relationship. She had also consulted colleagues who felt this would be a very helpful project. This time, I was writing a completely different book than the one I had begun years before. We have worked especially hard for the last two years despite being separated by continents and oceans.

We began by using pseudonyms. This felt safe and freed us both to write in a way that was true and uninhibited. Toward the end of writing, Seanne and I both felt that hiding behind false names did not serve the purpose of this book. This book is about truth. It is about vulnerability. It is my story, and for the long while that I could not and would not claim it, I was paralyzed. Using my real name in writing this is one of the most difficult things I have done, and yet, I feel it is more than just important; it is what I am called to do. Incest creates immense shame in families, shame that is crippling, especially for the victim. On the other hand, coming into the light of truth has been liberating; it has brought me more peace and freedom than I had before. Seanne and I hope this book will help free others from their own prisons of shame and fear.

The telling of this story in an open, honest manner outweighs my need for the protection of confidentiality. I made that clear to Seanne. However, using our real names is not only a personal matter but also a family issue. While we have maintained the integrity of our story, I have disguised my family and their details. I am sensitive to the fact that this story is painful for them and not every member of the family knows it. I also realize this story may be painful for any reader. I strongly recommend that you seek help if you notice you are triggered while reading it.

There is no chronology attempted in the narratives; the first chapter is of my father's funeral, years after my therapy with Seanne ended. Each chapter was written as daily incidents provided triggers to previous events. All names, except for ours, have been changed, as have places and details to give proper honor to people whose names are not important to the story.

A further note to readers: Had current laws been in place in the state of Nebraska, the law that now states uncategorically that the statute of limitations never runs out on sex offenders, I would not have sought therapy or told my story. I checked on this more than once before I began talking about my father. I was told that the statute of limitations had run out based on the laws at the time.

The format of our conversations is in plain text (my voice) and italics (Seanne's voice). Resources are included as footnotes where they are relevant.

There were many ethical issues I had to consider as I approached the idea of writing this book with Geri. I was bound by my professional Code of Ethics not to enter into a dual relationship with a client until a reasonable amount of time after therapy. Aside from that, the truth is that it took me a long while (and many consultations with professionals, both legal and those in my professional field) to sort out how the writing of this book could actually be possible at all.

Because our therapeutic relationship needed to end due to Geri's move abroad, her care needed to be transferred to a therapist in her new country of residence. Geri was indeed able to establish a good therapeutic relationship with a skilled psychologist in her new residence. She also utilized her extensive support network. Years passed, and she took a different teaching position at a university in another country.

It was some years after our therapeutic relationship ended that we began to casually communicate more frequently and resume discussions about her idea of the book. I was very busy during that time and did not have the ability to dedicate time to the project. I was also still ambivalent about doing it. I felt very uncomfortable thinking about commenting on the therapeutic process with a former client as well as contemplating the idea that these thoughts might one day be disclosed. Confidentiality defines the therapeutic relationship. Even though Geri, her mother, and other members of her family signed an informed consent to willingly disclose her story, it remains uncomfortable as a therapist to talk openly about a client relationship. The choice to use our real names was difficult for both of us, but we had numerous discussions in which Geri eventually convinced me it was necessary. It's a story about facing issues of shame and vulnerability. Using our real names means neither one of us can hide.

The managing of a relationship with a client requires much discernment. I have not found it easy. We are not allowed dual relationships with clients (for good reason), yet we also cannot abandon a client. (This was especially challenging to manage when Geri moved abroad.) I've attended many ethics trainings over the years where the complexity of practicing therapy is always underscored. Therapists, by their very nature, are caring individuals and vulnerable to blurring boundaries because of that. Yet, if boundaries are blurred too much, the role of therapist is contaminated and the client harmed as a result.

We began writing seven years after therapy ended. Geri and I were able to seamlessly move into a relationship as colleagues in the writing process. We made good use of Skype. We scheduled regular writing times, and I soon began to look forward to the discipline of writing with Geri. It became apparent to me how important it was for Geri to tell her story, to offer some redeeming value from her trauma by helping others with this writing.

The process of writing was painful at times, yet also surprisingly energizing. Geri has a wonderful sense of humor, and we were able to approach it all with a certain degree of lightness. We became very comfortable in our honesty with each other. We both mindfully worked at not slipping into the old hierarchical relationship of me as therapist, Geri as client. We wrote as colleagues. This was challenging at times when the material was difficult. However, Geri consistently had her own therapist during our time of writing, and we both maintained boundaries that respected this work. The mission of the book, to help others through our own transparency, sustained our motivation.

We hope anyone who reads this story, whether you are an incest victim, a professional, a family member, a friend of a victim, a mother or father of the victim, or a person who just wants to help and better understand, will find hope, help, and empowerment. If you are one who has been abused, I hope this work strengthens you to get the help you need so the cycle of hurt, pain, and shame can end or at least be better managed. If you are a therapist, I hope my lessons learned will help you be clearer in your own work with victims and their families.

This is intended to be a book designed to increase awareness, not to be in and of itself a self-help book. Nor is this intended to be a psychotherapy training manual. I selected my course of treatment based on my training at the time which was in person/client-centered methods as well as in solution-focused and trauma-informed care. I was heavily influenced by the work of Christine Courtois, PhD, who wrote, Healing the Incest Wound, Adult Survivors in Therapy, (Norton, 1988.). Since then she has other publications on treating complex trauma, rooted in relationship and and evidence-based approaches. I am Level II trained in EMDR and also draw heavily upon trauma-focused cognitive behavioral therapy. My core training is in family systems, which informs all my work. This book does not represent all that occurred during therapy. It is designed to offer a glimpse into the life of a victim of incest and a snapshot of her (and my experience with her) in therapy at that time.

Geri is very much a survivor. She was living the life of a victim before her healing journey began. It seemed like a long road before she could see herself as a survivor and live her life as such. This is the story of that road, the twists and turns it took, and the hope she has found along the way.

Geri Henderson & Seanne Emerton

2

Funeral

Looking at him lying there, at peace for the first time in his life no doubt, I knew that anything we'd shared, good or bad, was over. There was a feeling of complete separation and release that surprised me. I expected to feel something, seeing my father's body—at least, to sense a familiar dread and fear—but those feelings simply were not there. The lack of feeling, positive or negative, was another new experience. There was nothing more to fear, and I had no regret that our journey together had ended as it had. It was not the end that I had read about or was told is healthy for such relationships. There was no great apology, no dramatic separation, and no therapeutic confrontation. Just an end to what had been a terrible and long journey of struggle and hope.

(I have now realized, that there were many things that came to an end that day, but there are others that may never be as "complete" or finished as I had always hoped. I've always wanted a Good Housekeeping Seal of Approval: Congratulations! You're done! No. I guess not. My current therapist, Gretchen, after Seanne and Marilka, says she will never hand me that award.)

As this memoir is now written in retrospect, Geri is even clearer in her knowing that the healing journey is a lifetime effort. In fact, a significant factor in her healing is her ability to reflect and to continue to openly and honestly process her life experiences.

I had not really planned to come to the funeral. I had been abroad several years; the distance was long and the cost expensive. I thought I didn't care. I found out that was true; I didn't care, not really, not about saying goodbye to my father. But I was very glad I had come when I found out how much it meant to my siblings. I did all the things the eldest should do—be involved in the planning, organize the music, help choose flowers and casket, and agree to say something during the funeral. I told the only story I could think of where I'd been impressed with my father's kindness. It was on a snowy, bitter New Year's Eve when I left my parents' house to return to college in a car I'd just purchased. The clutch went out about two-and-a-half hours into my ten-hour trip. I called home. Despite having obligations as the minister of a conservative church, my father came, completely encased in a flannel-lined coverall. He'd roused a wrecking yard owner to find the spare part we needed, and he lay in the snow for several hours, fixing the car. It was hard for me to believe at the time, but it was an act of kindness and care that made a huge impression on me. When I finished telling my story at the funeral, I said something about having had a difficult relationship with Father and added my gratitude for the things he'd given me—a love of learning, a love of music, and an innate ability to teach.

He was not all "bad." He passed on many good qualities. It is important to identify the good and not completely reject the man. After all, Geri's father is part of her identity. We make a critical error when the father perpetrator is completely villainized. Doing so would have reinforced Geri's belief that she is indeed "bad" herself since she is her father's offspring.

Geri, perhaps because being first born but also perhaps because she is a person trained "to do the right thing," diligently maintained communication with her parents throughout her adult life. She would often entertain them for dinner in her home and suffer severe migraines for days afterward. Her father frequently wanted to sit by her at the dinner table. It took a great deal of coaching to have her assert her boundaries and sit away from him. She wouldn't hear of not inviting them to her home. The fact is that he was still her dad and family was still family. Early on, her brother and sister had no clue about what their father had done, and so Geri hosted family meals for the "greater good" and at the expense of herself and her own needs. In fact, her own needs were pushed so far down that she had no idea what they even were, let alone the voice to express them.

The art of therapy is to notice and hold the incongruences while press-ing the client to expand her conscious thought, to embrace the confusing spectrum of emotions. When I met Geri, she did not give herself permission to own her anger at her father—partly because of his good qualities and partly, I think, because her anger scared her. She had been trained to be the dutiful, first-born daughter. However, she could not effectively process the mixed bag of emotions from her abuse until she felt safe to own the anger she had toward him. To feel safe, Geri had to fully understand that expressing her anger did not mean rejecting her father completely. On some level, she loved him. Indeed, he had given her the gifts she articulated at his funeral: her love of learning, love of music, and the innate ability to teach. However, claiming anger toward her father and fully facing the reality that indeed he was a sexual perpetrator, has always been difficult for Geri.

I don't think I would have been able to trust Seanne had she initial-ly described me as a "dutiful daughter." It flew in the face of everything I knew. I had never thought of myself in that way but rather the "bad girl" my father had always told me I was. It would have been a surprise and not very helpful to have heard this from Seanne in the beginning, and I remember how long it took me to change my mind about this.

Timing is everything in therapy. I have to meet the client where she is and with high empathy. This is critical to helping the client feel safe. I con-stantly tuck away any hypotheses and must carefully edit my thoughts be-fore articulating them. The consequences of a poorly-timed statement from me could have been quite costly. I desperately wanted to reframe Geri as the dutiful daughter as early as the first session so she could begin feeling some compassion for herself. Yet, as she says, that would have flown in the face of her reality and would have discredited me. Doing therapy is like a chess game. I had to think through the impact of our next move and how Geri would most likely respond or take it in. The process is often frustratingly slow and requires great patience, which is challenging for me.

At my father's funeral it was the minister who made the biggest im-pression on everyone, even the family. He said, "I had a sermon prepared, but you have heard from his children and grandchildren more than I had planned to say. "

"However," he added, "what you should know is that toward the end of Charles' life, he became very concerned about the spiritual lives of those he saw—all the nurses, doctors, anyone who visited him. He clung to the cross of Jesus and wanted everyone to know of its importance. You see, Charles had done things that could have ripped his family apart. He was a deeply flawed man and knew the saving importance of redemption."

Behind me, I felt Seanne and all my closest friends take a breath. The minister then went on to let people know they could experience the same thing my father had: peace in redemption.

It was powerfully healing for Geri to have the minister publically recognize her father's flaws. The service itself embraced the dichotomies that defined Charles. This is an element of a well-designed service. The power of good ceremony cannot be overestimated. This service did more than extended therapy sessions could have for Geri's continued healing. This is because she could hear it claimed in a public place, and by a person she respected deeply, that truly her father was flawed. He wasn't a saint, and it was okay to say so. She didn't have to pretend anymore.

This funeral was five years after Geri terminated therapy with me. She had moved abroad and was seeing a therapist there at the time. Clearly her work in therapy was not complete. It helped me to know she had a therapist continuing to work with her on the incongruences of both loving and hating her father. At the time of her father's death, we had just begun working on this book and had renegotiated our relationship as colleagues. I chose to attend the funeral as her friend.

After the funeral, I spent another week with my family and found that we had all reacted to this event very differently. The relationships that my two younger siblings and I had with our father were very distinct from each other. This made our individual ways of saying goodbye to him very personal and also affected the way we each felt about his death and memorial service. I shouldn't have been surprised.

3

Why Didn't I Tell?

I had just visited my mother in the lovely assisted living center and had dinner with her and her friends that evening. My sister, Lily, planned to meet me for a visit. We went to our father's gravesite so I could see the monument we'd ordered the year before. Then, we went for some frozen yogurt and a chat. It had been over a year since we'd had a good chat, just the two of us. While we were talking, Lily's husband called and decided to join us. I've always enjoyed him and was glad to see him, too. He often adds great insight and a healthy sense of humor to our visits.

After the usual greetings and general catching up, Lily told me about their recent attendance at a conference. They had seen a number of people we knew from the childhood years we'd spent on the Pacific island of Norfolk while my parents were missionaries there. I think we all feel as though we've left parts of our hearts on that island, truly. We easily lapse into the local dialect, and we are always eager for news of our friends, still there. This code switching between American, British, and the island dialect was an unconscious linguistic negotiation we constantly performed, depending upon where we were. We now find ourselves deeply connected by the dialect we naturally use between us because it is often more expressive. Suddenly, Lily and George became serious and then said, "Geri, in spite of everything that's happened, so many people at the conference told us how grateful they are for what our folks did, especially our father."

"Yes, I know," I answered. "I came to terms with all of that when we all went back to the island several years ago. I realized that God used Father to help others because he was willing and available. God used a donkey, too, once. I'm okay with hearing that people appreciated my parents' work. The dichotomy of what I experienced and what others say doesn't really bother me much anymore. As a matter of fact, I'm glad to know that there was real value in what Mother and Father did there. Somehow, all of the horrible experiences I have had seem less important because I have accepted the fact that the greater good was being served. I still say there are good, very good reasons for having kept our home life a secret. There were much bigger issues at stake than just the happiness of one (or three) children." They nodded.

"Oh no," I think as I read this. "Don't believe her!" I want to shout. The many problems Geri has had throughout her life are because she endured the abuse so long and was not protected. Is the "greater good" really worth that?

I know this isn't exactly what therapists want to hear but, for me, it makes a great deal of sense. I realize how much would have been lost had Mother or I told what we knew about Father (even if what we knew were very different versions of what happened). My younger siblings, for whom I've always cared a great deal and whose relationship with our father was better, would probably have lost their father. Beyond our family, people who believed in my parents and what they were doing would have felt betrayed, spiritually lost. No, I was sure it was not worth jeopardizing all of that to have told the secret.

Does what happened in my house make all my parents' work less important? Or does it seem that what happened in my house makes everything they did for people a sham? I don't think so. As a result of their work, teaching, and influence, people's lives were changed for the better. I cannot claim any altruistic motive for keeping the secret, but, in hindsight, I'm glad I did. Might people discount my claims to increased health and peace? Perhaps. The chapter on "Shame" speaks to the importance of disclosure and the terrible effects of long-term silence.

Geri and I frequently asked ourselves who would she be today had she told? Would her resiliency be as richly developed? Would she be as sensitive to others? Would Geri have the keenly-developed emotional intelligence traits of self-awareness, problem solving, and adaptability that she has now if she had told early on? How would the stress on the family have played out had she told? Should that matter? Would she have received the care she needed had she told? Would good therapists have been available to her to help her sort out the complexity of feelings she had? If she had told, would she have been spared more of the emotional trauma? Would she have been raped? Would she have had a more successful career, having been able to engage in it earlier and with more clarity, without the myriad of emotional and physical issues that have impeded her in many ways?

We will never really know. But because she didn't tell, she has had years of suffering, including difficulty with setting boundaries, difficulty with going out in public, not to mention a multitude of physical issues resulting from the stress on her adrenal glands. Her body suffered more than just the abuse. As a child, she had severe eczema. Today, she has vascular issues, many allergies, obesity, migraines, and depression. Her body's stress response became activated at a young age.

"Over time, repeated activation of the stress response takes a toll on the body....and contributes to high blood pressure, promotes the formation of artery-clogging deposits, and causes brain changes that may contribute to anxiety, depression and addiction......as well as obesity, both through direct mechanisms, causing people to eat more, or indirectly, decreasing sleep and exercise." "Understanding the Stress Response."[1]

Geri's problem with obesity is not uncommon in women who have experienced sexual abuse. The weight is often a "protective measure" against being seen as sexually attractive. Additionally, obesity perpetuates the shame cycle, in which she was entrapped.

Geri was suicidal more than once. Would she have been susceptible to chronic suicidal ideation had she told? Who would have believed her? The Department of Health and Human Resources did not exist in that time, and in the country where she resided. Resources were indeed limited. And there was virtually no campaign of educational messages encouraging children of abuse to tell. Further, by Geri not telling, the anger toward her father as a child sexual abuse perpetrator was displaced—onto herself. It wasn't

---

1   "Understanding the Stress Response", March 2011. *Harvard Health Publications*, Harvard Medical School

expressed at the one responsible for the abuse. This continues to be an issue for Geri today.

In the course of finishing this book, my family and I helped gather documents, slides, and letters for a history of the organization for which my father worked. I have learned more about my father from people who knew him as a tireless problem-solver, someone whose influence in Norfolk continues even now. The incongruences Seanne mentioned have become more puzzling with what I have learned. Still, there are new things I've discovered that give me a kind of peace about my father's many good qualities.

4

Dr. Elizabeth Mahlou

A close friend of mine travels all over the world. She was coming to the city, an hour away from where I spent my summer vacations. I picked her up from the airport, and we went to dinner. I have to say, she is an amazing person on so many levels. She has survived some horrible childhood experiences herself, and not only survived them, but came through them and built a happy, successful life, both personally and professionally. Like she says, she's an incurable optimist, and she really never thought of herself as a victim of her parents or grandfather. Rather, she saw herself as a fighter for all of her seven younger siblings.

This story of Geri's friend speaks to the power of resilience that seems inherent in some. Thank goodness Geri has some of this resiliency, too, and has always seen herself as a fighter/survivor and has not over-identified as "victim." While she has resiliency, she has also been prone to denying problems. Avoidance has been a well-developed, albeit ultimately ineffective, coping and defense mechanism for her. Avoidant behavior is often a byproduct of Post-Traumatic Stress Disorder, which was one of Geri's diagnoses.

Dr. Mahlou looked at me and said, "I'm so glad you're finally getting around to writing this story. I feel it has been important for a long time."

Then, she went on to ask me about how Seanne and I would handle the necessary honesty we must have in our writing. For example, would I be honest about the things that had frustrated me or made me angry? I told her that I thought that part would be fairly easy because Seanne already knew what most of those things were. Of course, I can be much more open and express my feelings more readily and clearly since I don't have to worry about how that might be interpreted in a therapeutic relationship.

Then I told Elizabeth this story:

We had been working together for some time in therapy when Seanne suggested that having a meeting with my mother would be very helpful. I remember exactly how I felt the first time she suggested it—I was shocked. It was virtually impossible to continue working that day, and I could think of nothing else the following week. I couldn't believe it would be helpful, and I knew for sure it would hurt my mother. If it hurt my mother, it would hurt me, too. I had worked so hard and so long to avoid that very thing.

The time my father hurt my mother (the only time I knew about then) I could hardly forgive him. No matter how many years have passed, I can still remember seeing my mother, sitting all alone, crying in church. Seeing that, a very rare occurrence back then, made me very sad. When I found out the reason for her tears, Father's confession that he'd touched me inappropriately, I was very angry with him.

Now, my therapist was suggesting I should do something similar, as I understood it. How could she? I thought, "If she really cares about how I feel, she will not make me do this."

Over time, and after talking to a couple of friends, I realized that I may have to agree—if only to get my closest friends and Seanne to shut up. I grew tired of hearing how much a meeting with mother would help and fighting everyone who knew about it (probably no more than three or four people really). Whether they truly believed it would help or even knew why, they had great faith in Seanne. They always did. When one of my closest friends said she would drive ten hours north to be with me, take me, and stay with me for an extra day afterward, I caved in to the pressure and agreed even though I remained convinced that everyone was very, very wrong.

OK! Fine! Between the time I said okay and the appointment, I went through a miserable time—very angry at Seanne and everyone else–very sad that after this I would have no relationship at all with my mother, the only parent who'd really loved me. Even as I write this, I remember the terror leading up to that evening meeting. The night before, my sister and two friends said prayers for the meeting. It probably helped them, but I was in a complete panic and wished desperately I might die within the next 24 hours.

(Even with all the time that has passed, when I look back on this time, I can easily feel the fear all over again. It's weird because I know what the outcome was, and yet, I still hate the pain it caused my mother and the terror it caused me. I don't think there is any way to convey this properly in words. With a previous therapist, Pamela, I had been pushed to go to the Menninger Clinic, then in Topeka, Kansas. As we began the process leading up to my going there, I was completely shocked that Menninger's wanted access to my parents and even wanted them to come for the first week! Of course, my father refused, saying he couldn't leave his work for that long, but Mother agreed. Later, one of my friends would remark, "Geri, I've never seen anyone work so hard and so fast to get Pamela to change her mind. Indeed! I didn't go, mainly because of the length of time required, the lack of proper insurance, and the panic about meeting my mother there.)

Geri had not shared with me this earlier attempted intervention. It may or may not have been helpful for me to have known about her failed attempt for family therapy at Menninger's. All I knew was that Geri was terrified, but I had to stay my course. I had to trust myself and my training that this was indeed the best course of action to take at the time. Geri was ready for it therapeutically even though she expressed only fear and panic. She was also highly skilled in manipulative maneuvers and used every possible trick in the book to wiggle out of doing it—even pulling the suicidal card.

Come on! I didn't do that, did I? OK, I probably did.

I had to assess for risk, of course. And I had to read through the lines to determine real risk versus manipulation, especially when Geri talked of or implied suicide. (Geri had some active Borderline Personality Disorder, BPD[2], traits complicating the picture. Symptoms often include "frantic efforts to avoid real or imagined abandonment" [DSM-V] and can lead to perceived manipulative behaviors in a desperate attempt not to feel abandoned.) I felt her behaviors at this point were primarily aimed at getting out of doing the session. She wanted to run away.

---

2   BPD is a mental health disorder that generates significant emotional instability, where often the person has a distorted self-image and feels fundamentally flawed. http://www.mayoclinic.org/diseases-conditions/borderline-personality-disorder/basics/definition/con-20023204

Of course, it would not have been clinically sound to do this family therapy intervention without Geri's support system intact, which included her very loyal friends and her highly skilled and caring brother-in-law. With Geri's permission, I contacted her pastor and her brother-in-law who knew the history and were close to both Geri and her mother. I needed to verify that her mother not only would be able to handle this session but also would most likely be appropriate with Geri. Of course, there was no guarantee of this outcome, but it required installing as many safety measures as possible and then trusting in the process. After also getting reassurance that Geri would have the needed support after the session, I began preparing Geri for the session as best I could by discussing with her the "outline" of the session, clarifying her intentions and my intentions and reassuring her I would do all in my power to keep her and her mother safe.

Again, with Geri's permission, I called her mother who lived in another city. Without going into any detail, I tried to prepare her as much as possible. She was already aware that Geri was in therapy so I simply said the time had come where I needed her presence to help Geri move forward. I reassured her mother that my intention was to create a safe place so that both Geri and she could be honest and that the hope was their relationship would deepen as a result. She graciously agreed to come.

Seanne arranged the meeting for after hours, when the office would be completely quiet and deserted. That evening, my dear brother-in-law brought Mother to the office. That was one thing I'd requested. I wanted to be sure that after our session, she would not be alone but would have someone she loved and who loved and respected her close by. I knew that it was impossible to expect my father to do anything to help anyone, even his wife, with any part of this issue. My friend brought me to the office and waited with my brother-in-law. I heard they had a good chat.

I remember being completely petrified. I took the chair farthest away from both of them, focused on my breathing, and had to use all my self-control not to cry. I did not want this to be a time when Mother would reach out to me because she felt sorry for me. Besides, I was quite sure that the first tears would lead to a complete waterfall, tears that would never, ever end. I couldn't allow that to happen. I felt like my life and sanity depended on the complete control I was determined to maintain.

I was aware of Geri's stance and understood it, yet was concerned that she would not allow herself to be real and vulnerable for the session. That session felt like a juggling act as I attempted to support yet push Geri. I wanted and needed to care for and support her mother as well while pushing for honesty and true listening on both their parts. Mostly, I wanted Geri to feel heard by her mother and to finally feel supported by her. Geri had spent her life protecting others and putting herself last. During this session, she needed to receive.

Seanne began. I cannot remember what she said because I was so scared. It was impossible to concentrate on what she was saying. We had talked ahead of time about what was okay to say and what was not. I didn't think my mother needed to hear the details of my sexual abuse. Mother thought she knew, and, unless she asked, I didn't want her to have to know more. I thought (and still think) that the degree of abuse is not as important as the effect it has and the way it is interpreted.

(I agree with Geri here. Even though someone may not have experienced the degree of sexual abuse Geri had or endured the long length of time that the abuse occurred, I have seen many clients who have been quite traumatized from a single incident of sexual abuse that consisted of fondling and not penetration.)

I heard Seanne say something about asking for the meeting because I needed to hear some things from my mother. I thought, "No! I do not!" but, unable to hear my thoughts, she pressed on. She told Mother that I always thought I was a terrible girl, someone who'd deserved all that had happened and that I continued to believe I was a bad person. She said more, but I can't remember it. What I do remember very well, though, was my mother's response: She cried. Sobbing, she said, "I thought Geri was perfect and begged her father not to beat her. When I got married, I promised myself that our home would be happy, our children well-loved and treated gently, not like the home I grew up in that was strict and harsh."

Then, she said, "It didn't turn out that way at all! Her father thought he knew best, and I could not argue or defy his will. I felt bad for the way she was treated. She was such a good girl, and what he interpreted as willful misbehavior, I knew were her attempts to be helpful—the behavior of a child who was trying to do the right thing. I knew that a quiet word was all she needed to be corrected. He didn't need to whip her."

By now, Mother was completely lost in her tears. She could hardly speak.

Despite my mother's tears, my attempts to remain cool and distant were mostly successful, at least as far as I could tell. I appeared calm on the outside though I was having trouble breathing and my stomach was in knots. What my mother said dumbfounded me. I could hardly believe it! She thought I was perfect! Wow! It was so hard to wrap my head around that news. It simply didn't match anything I thought I knew about myself. I was stunned. Could it be possible that she had not agreed with my father—that she did not think of me as the naughtiest child she'd ever known? What a relief this would be!

Yes, this was very powerful for Geri to hear, and it was something only her mother could have said to her so that she could really "get it."

Despite my state of shock, I knew there was still a part of the conversation left to come, perhaps the hardest part. I don't remember how it was brought up. (Did mother say, "And when he told me he'd touched her...." or did Seanne ask Mother all she knew?) I do remember I held my breath and started to get a headache. Then, I heard Seanne say, "There was more, much more."

Mother didn't ask what more there was, but she cried more tears. She probably suspected she hadn't known everything, only what he had told her. We suddenly realized, in shock, that he'd lied to both of us. At the point that my father's secret visits to my room came to an end, he told me that he'd confessed to my mother and apologized to her. He said there was no need for me to talk to her. What he told my mother was that he'd "touched me inappropriately" and promised not to do it again. Then, he told her that she didn't need to talk to me. Following his instructions, neither one of us had spoken about this with each other for over 30 years. In these years of silence, I believed my mother had been blaming me while she believed she had the whole story. I realize now that I have always been angrier with him for hurting my mother than I was for his hurting me. The other thing I realize is that my main reason for not wanting her to know was because I didn't want her to blame me. When he told her, he had implicated me. I felt horribly guilty.

Of course, this is another reason this session with Geri's mother was so vital to her healing process. There is no way that I, as Geri's therapist, could have cleared up this misunderstanding in the same way that the words from

Geri's mother did. When they both realized that Geri's father had lied to each of them, there was a wellspring of forgiveness and understanding for each other that filled the room.

Blessedly, our meeting, an hour and a half long, came to an end and mother left. Seanne and I stayed together a few more minutes, but I have no memory of what she said. Mostly, I remember blaming her for Mother's terrible distress, and, at that point, I could not see that there was going to be any benefit at all in what had been said and heard. I just wanted out. I needed to leave. I think it was probably obvious to anyone else that this meeting was one of the several turning points in my healing, a fact I've had to admit and even thank Seanne for arranging, as difficult as it was to say it aloud.

After hearing this story, my friend Elizabeth was satisfied that our writing would, indeed be honest—but, even now, it's not easy. No, it's very difficult to lay it on the line and to say it in a way that is both transparent and clear.

While this session was only an hour and a half long, it required extensive preparation ahead of time. Of course, a therapist never really knows how a session will go, even with the best preparation in place. But this session could have easily backfired and made things worse for Geri. Preparation included not only preparing the participants individually, as best as possible, but carefully thinking through the sequence of topics needing to be addressed. The session had to have a solid opening, middle, and closing with all parties feeling heard and safe to express themselves as well as to listen to each other. I had to have clarity on where the session needed to go/ the desired outcome, without being attached to the outcome because it was, after all, the client's session.

The timing had to be right, and both Geri and her mother had to be in "as-good-as-it-gets" states of mind in order for this to be successful. I had a certain urgency about doing this session considering Geri's mother's health and age and considering that Geri was not going to stay in the area forever. This kind of session is impossible to manage effectively either on the phone or online as it requires intense observation, reading non-verbal communication, and the ability to "sit with" some highly charged moments. It required that I orchestrate, yet not control. I had clear therapeutic goals and objectives, yet the language and participation of the players in the room make all the difference in the outcome. I had to first create an environment where Geri and her mother felt safe. This means I needed to be extremely mindful of my actions and words—things like my use of language, timing, and my body posture. I needed to stay in the moment and listen deeply, showing care and empathy for both. I had a lot of anxiety about this session, so I was concerned I would be able to stay present with the process, and not worried about what I would do next.

(I have always been able to count on Seanne's empathy, sensitivity, and control. I knew, at my core, I could trust her to take good care of both of us. Hearing now how much she worked to prepare does not surprise me. What does surprise me is her description of the balancing act. I could never have guessed. She was "tough" so that I came to believe I did not have many more options for moving forward, and she made her role look easy. That created enough trust to agree to the meeting.)

It was highly important, for instance, that Geri's mom not feel ganged up on, but that she feel I had some empathy for her role and her position. This was challenging for me. Because I had intimately walked the journey with Geri, bearing witness to her emotional scars and wounds, part of me was angry with her mother for not "getting it" and for not protecting Geri. Effective family therapy, however, requires that the therapist manage her own feelings so she can understand various family members' perspectives.

Understanding does not mean "agreeing with." If Geri's mother had felt I judged her or sensed that I was angry with her, it would have shut down the session. Geri would have taken the position of rescuing her mother, and therapeutic work would have been blocked. So, the biggest challenge as therapist in this case was to manage myself and to be aware of my own feelings. I then had to stay clear and keep the focus. This is why the therapist cannot also be a friend to the client. A friend would be much more likely to be seduced by the client's perspective and want to overly protect the client, without clarity for the larger picture.

Only recently have I discovered how difficult it is for me to be grateful to anyone who acts for my greater good in full knowledge that it will hurt. I cannot describe how strongly I feel about avoiding hurt—mine or anyone else's, even those who hurt me. The fact that someone I trust pushes me toward pain, to push me *through* pain to a rewarding result makes me angry. But, "rewarding" is really the only way to describe what followed.

5

Mother

As I wrote about the meeting with Mother in Seanne's office, I relived the anger, frustration, and sadness that had so enveloped me during that whole experience. Without a doubt, it was one of the most difficult sessions in years of therapy. In reliving those feelings, it became difficult to think beyond that. Now that retelling is finished, I realize that I didn't talk much about how worthwhile that session has been in the long run.

Yes, I would agree that it was a most difficult session. I had to trust myself in knowing that "the push" was not only needed but that the timing was right. I always risk being fired by the client under normal circumstances, and especially during these times. So it was a calculated roll of the dice. I knew, however, that not to push Geri therapeutically would mean she would very likely wallow in depression the rest of her life. Not only was I leaning on my training and best evidence-based practice methods then, but I also had strong intuition that this was the time for this intervention.

Intuition cannot be discounted in the therapeutic relationship. Like other therapists, I can get so caught up in the cognitive/cerebral world of therapy practice that I may discount or not trust my inner, intuitive knowing. The self of the therapist takes constant work so that inner knowing is as clear as possible and the risk of projections upon the client of the therapist's own issues are minimized. This is an ethical responsibility to our clients and demands disciplined self-care, working on one's own family of origin issues and good peer supervision.

As therapist, I need to be aware of my own non-verbal communication during the session, my stance, posture ("Do I lean in now or sit back?"), my breathing, the words I speak and the timing of those words, as well as track-ing each person in the room with his/her words and non-verbal communi-cation. All of this needs to occur while I simultaneously keep the focus on the ultimate goal of the session: watching for windows of opportunity to weave and direct interactions appropriately. I don't always succeed.

Just reading this makes me tired! I'm grateful Seanne knew how to take care of herself and both of us, but, under those conditions, it's mind-blow-ing that anyone can. I understand what she says about self-care being an ethical element. I couldn't do it, of course. Seanne once gave me a book on self-care. It made me angry. It took me a long time to be able to pick up the book and longer to read any part of it. What Seanne writes about being absolutely clear with who you are as a therapist makes me think of it as a drowning rescue. She had to be like a lifeguard who was completely unhin-dered, strong enough to keep swimming while carrying those of us who have fallen overboard, fully clothed, weighed down by all sorts of useless extra baggage. I think only the strongest, most determined lifeguard would have been able to rescue me safely.

Thank God, Geri was willing to be rescued. Yes, she resisted at times, but she really didn't want to drown. Geri, at her core, had and has the will to live and to live fully. Her passion for her work and her strong relationships with others, as well as her personal faith, are huge strengths that made her "rescue-able" and increase her ability to be resilient.

Without a doubt, this session was one of the most helpful. Mother and Father had made a kind of pact never to disagree in front of the children; I knew that. But for the first time, I heard that she hadn't believed that I was naughty, troublesome, rude, and all the other things Father used to tell me. For the first time, I was able to hear, in a way I never had before, that I was okay and not the worst child and person she'd ever known. How otherwise could I have ever known that her silence during his accusations had not been tacit agreement?

My long-suffering friends and therapists had tried hard to give me positive messages for years, all without success. I simply could not allow myself to hear it. I always thought and sometimes even said, "My father, who knew me best, thought I was an awful person. You do not know me like he did. You cannot know what he knew about me." That had always been the end of many discussions, discussions that must have been irritating, frustrating, and hopeless for the wonderful people who had the patience to call me "friend." I could never understand how the awful person I was had such an amazing array of incredible friends. I was convinced I had not deserved even one of them, much less a wealth of such people in my life.

But Seanne had made me listen to my mother.

Yes! This is precisely the point.

My mother also knew me best, and she had thought I was perfect! This was news so stunning I could hardly believe it. It took a long time for my mind to adjust to this. I had to learn to live with a new me—a person I hardly knew. Could I even learn to love this new me someday? I remember a time when even writing those words would make me cry. Earlier, in therapy, efforts to get me to look at pictures of the child I had been were almost futile. I would have a momentary understanding that I would never blame any *other* child for what had happened to them but for Geri, the child? Impossible. I had hated her for "what she had done," for what had resulted in hospital stays, multiple trials of antidepressants, and, worst of all, the hours of embarrassing and painful truth-telling therapy I had to undergo.

That child[2] was an easy target for everything about my life I'd come to hate, all having to do with the necessity of attempting to get well, a necessity imposed on me when I hardly cared most of the time. Now, I would have to reconsider everything I had known and accepted without question about this girl. Mother had said otherwise. It must be so. Still, it was difficult. I replayed her words over and over in my head. How long did it take for me to recognize that, with all my faults, with all that child's faults, I had been a good child? I don't know but, over time, I felt I could learn to accept it.

Despite the clarification that came from the session with her mother, Geri continued to feel extreme shame and blame for her abuse. I believed we needed to move forward with some forgiveness toward her inner child in order to release some of the contempt she held. This was hard to do because she resisted placing the blame squarely where it belonged: on her father.

Instead, "little Geri" got it all. This fed her shame/blame cycle, keeping her virtually stuck in her old behavior patterns (including her symptoms of borderline personality disorder and her tendencies toward dissociation).

I know Geri as a person who has remarkable relationships with the students she has taught. She truly loves children. So, I thought a natural therapeutic intervention would be to love her own "inner child," for whom she felt such contempt. As I'd anticipated, it was very off-putting to Geri when I first broached the subject. I invited her to bring to therapy a picture of herself as a child. She nearly vomited at the suggestion. However, she did follow through. (She was a "dutiful client" in many ways.)

We utilized guided imagery as a tool to picture herself in her safe place with her inner child, nurturing her and meeting her as she was. We used this tool frequently in therapy until I observed some movement on Geri's part toward compassion for the child part of her. This piece of the work may have helped a little. I'm not really sure.

In fact, being a therapist is the most humbling job on the planet. One never really knows how a client is moving forward, or really if they are. We like to pretend we know, and, of course, we like to pretend we are the reason that clients "get better." We have evidence-based interventions and measurements to justify progress and to justify our existence, but therapy is really a very small part of a client's world. The power of healing is really outside the therapy room—in the relationships and experiences clients have. Hopefully, therapy helps enhance these relationships.

I guess I would add that I continued to look at the pictures I had from age four, hoping that I would see something lovable there or that I would recognize her without hating her. It was easy to believe that she had behaviors and an appearance that caused her father to treat her as he had. But, the truth is, I kept thinking about her, long after Seanne and I had stopped working together. I still think about her, and, now that I've gained some self-confidence and self-belief, try to connect with her. I still work at loving her, but sometimes, I think it's okay we are separated. I feel very differently from the little girl. Very. I know I would never blame another child for what has happened to them. Therefore, it makes no sense to keep blaming little Geri.

Other amazing pieces of information revealed in that session were the lies Mother and I had believed. I believed that my father had been truthful with Mother when he'd said to me, "I've told your mother what I did and apologized." I believed then that she knew all that had happened but never spoke to me about it because she blamed me. I thought I understood and accepted the fact that "it" was a closed topic forever. At our joint session with Seanne, Mother realized she'd been lied to as well. That was clear. The understanding that we'd been separated from each other for thirty years by my father's lies came as a shock to both of us.

Since, without telling her specifics, Mother and I have had several conversations about our perceptions of what did or did not happen. While there has never been anything as dramatic in its revelations or effects as that first meeting, it has been a relief for both of us that we can talk openly and honestly about almost anything.

As Mother has aged, our relationship has shifted a bit. I watch her as she becomes more forgetful, sometimes repeating embarrassing stories to her friends about her children. As an adult, I am finally able to give her the kind of relationship she has wanted—the fun, teasing sort of relationship that she tried so hard to have when we were growing up. I am not hurt or upset by her teasing the way I was as a child. Instead, I am teasing her in return in the way she likes, the way that makes her laugh and feel that someone knows her well enough to enjoy that kind of relationship with her. I believe it is the kind of relationship she had with her father, a man who showed his love through his playful teasing, someone she has probably missed.

This is the gift of Geri having done her emotional work and, of course, her mother's willingness to show up and be honest. The last stage of her mother's life can now be fully embraced and enjoyed by both Geri and her mother.

These happy endings are not always possible, of course. It's not unusual for cutoffs to occur with the victim of abuse and the mother. This most often occurs when the mother does not acknowledge the abuse in any manner and persists in denial, showing no empathy or compassion for her child. Clearly, that was not the case with Geri's mother. Based on my conversations with Geri's support system, I knew I could trust this about her mother prior to the joint session. Her mother's ability to listen, clarify, and support Geri during this difficult session paved the way for Geri to be able to truly do her hard work.

It was not immediate, but I slowly began to feel that what Seanne was asking me to do and what I was trying to do could produce real benefits. It took me awhile to overcome my resentment of being pushed so hard, but when I did and saw what I had learned, it was much easier to trust the process and follow the path as Seanne continued to point the way.

If Geri were a parent, the work she did in this session and throughout her therapy, would be the best gift she could give her children. To not do the work would almost guarantee the repeat of old, dysfunctional patterns. Even though Geri is not a parent, the work Geri and her mother did was a multi-generational gift. Because there is no more secrecy and because healthy dialogue is now possible, Geri's family has been healed on many levels. This doesn't mean that every member of Geri's extended family needs to be told what happened. The power is in the fact that Geri herself has not kept this secret and has been transparent with her mother, siblings, and in-laws. Therefore, her work has a ripple effect that permeates the family system in a very healthy way. That's not to say that this alone creates a "functional family." However, it significantly contributes to healthy patterns which have the ability to repair and heal.

As we will see, Geri's honest, hard work resulted in the reduction of her borderline personality disorder symptoms. It also significantly reduced her symptoms of depression and post-traumatic stress disorder to the point that she could live and work abroad.

Perhaps there was just a window of time that made such a meeting possible—a tiny window allowing me to be present to watch a lady of grace and love reach out to her eldest daughter for a time of mutual healing. Earlier, I was not ready. Later would have been too late.

Yes, it is about seizing that window. I credit Geri's highly competent support group with her ability to lean forward in courage and faith.

Many years later, I find myself back in therapy with Gretchen, the new therapist Seanne recommended, trying to deal with this. I do not hate the girl now, but I don't have any particular feelings of compassion for her either. It is a difficult piece that I have trouble even wrapping my head around. Learning to love and have empathy for the child I was feels like such a highly abstract concept at times. On the other hand, continuing to hold her at arm's length so I can ignore her hurt is not a good solution either. It would sadden my mother to think that the child she apparently adored has grown up to hate herself so much.

Geri Henderson & Seanne Emerton

6

Lies and Secrets

When I think about the lies my father told and all the unsaid thoughts and fears that were part of the air we breathed at our house, I remember a particularly frightening time when the truth was almost brought into the open many, many years before that session in Seanne's office.

Mother and Father had come for my college graduation—a ceremony I had attempted to forego, perhaps to avoid having them come. But that same weekend my cousin had planned his wedding to coincide with the gathering of the families and friends for our combined graduations. I was involved in the wedding preparations, and Mother decided to ride along with me to a nearby city for the rehearsal. The truth was, she had an agenda that I couldn't have imagined. If I'd had any idea of her intention, I'd have been even more frightened and much more uncomfortable.

I sometimes had nightmares about Mother dying and me being forced to marry my father to look after my younger siblings and keep the family functioning "normally." I always awoke crying and grateful it had not come true yet though I clearly continued to think about it when I awoke. Even though I realized that Mother was all that stood between me and my being completely subsumed by my father, her presence made me feel guilty and uncomfortable.

This speaks well to the conflicted and complex feelings so common in incest survivors. Geri loves her mother fully and, while she didn't protect

Geri from the abuse, her mother did buffer the relationship Geri had with her dad. Yet, she can't help feeling guilty and uncomfortable around her, making an emotionally intimate relationship impossible and causing great emotional stress in Geri.

After riding together for several minutes, my mother said, "One of your professors told me to ask you if something happened to you in Norfolk because you do not seem to allow any of the boys interested in you to get close to you. Did you tell her about your father?"

It's interesting that it took this outside interventionist (the professor) to inquire before Geri's mother brought the subject up. The unspoken rule in the family system was, as Geri said, to not talk about it. It was the norm to exist in an environment rife with unsaid thoughts and fears. This dynamic, common in families where abuse is present, contributes even more to the victim's reluctance to speak out and tell.

When Geri first told me that her mother asked, "Did you tell them about your father?" my initial reaction was anger toward her mother. These words confirmed her knowledge about the abuse though she had never broached the topic until now. Why is that? Does it mean her mother didn't really love her? On the contrary, Geri's mother seems to love her very much. So much so, she had to deny the truth to herself because it was too much for her to fully accept.

The role of the mother in the father/daughter incest dynamic is highly complex. The mother is in an impossible situation, especially if she is trapped in the marriage. There are myriad reasons why women are trapped in such marriages. Financial and emotional dependence are primary. It was further complicated in this case because Geri's father was a religious public figure, and the family lived abroad. Living abroad contributed to the isolation of the family system, which is another common factor in abusive families. The shame that would befall the family, should it become public, was too great a risk. This all contributed to the conditions of secrecy. So, while it's common to feel anger toward the mother who doesn't protect, it is important as a clinician to override that anger and look at the big picture.

I was nonplussed, totally puzzled by my mother's question about my father! I had not thought consciously about what he had done for many years. As a matter of fact, I never spent conscious time thinking about it while living through it even though every daily and nightly habit had been circumscribed by my need to somehow take control of what was going on, to be in charge in some way. Why was she asking me whether or not I'd told about my father? It took me a few seconds to register what she could have meant.

"No," I said, "of course not!" I was indignant. If I didn't or wouldn't think about it, why would I have said anything to anyone else? At this moment, I prayed for some sort of divine or any other kind of intervention. Oh, please, please, please, let's not talk about this! Please!

Mother continued, "Did something else happen?"

As a matter of fact, something else *had* happened. How could I tell her what had happened? In some measure, as time passed, I'd come to blame her for the rape I had endured more than four years earlier.

This is astute self-awareness on Geri's part: the fact that she was aware of blaming her mother for the rape that she had experienced. It's not unusual for the victim to protect the mother from all blame. It's healthy, at least, that Geri could see the contextual relationship within which the rape occurred, not that her mother was indeed responsible for the rape.

I had returned to the island at 17, after the year of American high school on the East Coast that my mother had insisted on. The American co-ed high school experience had so terrified me that I'd begged to return home.

My Norfolk high school had ended with the award of a Cambridge Certificate of General Education. "O" Level, allowing me to teach in a Norfolk elementary school for the upcoming year, and that's what I did for the next year.

It was a wild experience, without textbooks or curriculum. I read everything I could about educating small children. Each night, I spent hours preparing twenty-five individual copybooks for each child. The age range and grade levels of the children were all so different.

There was an American working there, doubling as an office manager and Vice Principal, and we became close friends over time. When she had to leave the island for a conference, she asked me to stay at her house in the evenings to be with her children, two girls I really liked. Another friend of hers would provide a chauffeur to take us to and from school and various other after-school activities.

I began this story and told my mother that I didn't know that the Vice Principal's friend also paid for the house, the maid, tuition for the children's private schools, and other things too. He began to come over in the evenings, have dinner with us, and always ended his evening with his own concoction, a dreadful tasting rum, lime, and coffee mix.

I reminded my mother of the one afternoon, back at my parents' house, when I had said, "Mother, I'm worried about Easton. He comes over every evening and drinks and touches me."

(At the time, she had said, "I've told you how to handle that," to which I had not responded, realizing that whatever it was she thought she'd told me, I could not remember. I had searched my mind. What could it be? My mind had started spinning and finally stopped, devoid of answers.)

Often, because mothers of abuse victims feel like failures, they project their feelings of inadequacy onto their victim child by blaming the child. Here, the words, "I've told you how to handle that," may have implied that Geri had control over the situation and that it was her fault if the situation got out of hand. At least, that is how Geri reported she felt about this comment. But how can we really know? Maybe Geri's mother's comment of "I've told you how to handle that" was out of concern and nothing more. It's likely that her mother felt quite helpless to really assist Geri. This is a good example of communication that needs to be clarified. Yet, at the time, Geri did not have the skill set to assertively inquire of her mother what she meant by that statement.

The next time Easton came over he said, "Has Patti [the Vice Principal] written?"

I said, "Yes. I'll get the letter."

"No, no hurry," he replied. "Get the children to bed first."

I did that and then walked down the hallway to Patti's bedroom where I'd been sleeping. Not bothering to turn on the light, I reached for the letter on the bureau. As I touched the letter, Easton came up behind me, grabbed me, and dragged me over to the bed. It was impossible for me to imagine that I could cry out or scream with the children sleeping so close by. What feels embarrassing to relate is that it took so little effort on his part, after my initial struggle. What was clear to me then was that my father was right—I was a terrible girl and that fact must be obvious to Easton or anyone else who wanted me. He left his watch on the bureau. When I saw it, I thought, "Whore!"

Easton later promised that he would not be so rough the next time. He said I would even grow to enjoy it. He had everything planned. He would pay for a nice duplex beside his mother's home. That way, no one would know he was visiting me.

Further, in the twisted mind of this man, he'd done me a huge favor by having sex with me. As a "return favor," he asked me to get the contract for his furniture manufacturing company to make the church pews in the new church my father was building. I appeared to acquiesce, and there were times I let myself believe that there was nothing better for me in this life. I should be grateful to have anyone care about me even if it was this way. After all, father had always said, "I'm teaching you about love." This was probably the best I could ever hope to have. I remember that Easton was obsessed with the pop song, Angel of the Morning, that had just come out that spring. He called it our song. Feeling trapped, I told my parents I wanted to stay in Norfolk Island. "What? Not go to college?" "No. Not now, anyway."

After two weeks, Patti came home, and I couldn't help but tell her my story. Thankfully, it was nearing the end of the school year, so the fact that my disclosure ruined our friendship and Patti's relationship with Easton didn't matter too much in the long run.

Obviously, Patti and my mother had had a chat, about which I reminded Mother because back then she had told me, "Patti says you must get off this island and go to college. It would be a terrible, dreadful waste. We cannot let you stay."

It's not uncommon for untreated victims of sexual abuse to have few, if any, boundaries. It's as if they have radar emanating from them that says, "Abuse me." Perpetrators easily pick up on it either consciously or subconsciously. This perpetuates the cycle of abuse and continues the victim's belief that they are, indeed "bad." It sets up a shame cycle, where behaviors continue to happen that keep the untreated victim in the feeling state of shame because this is what feels normal to them. By the time Geri recounted this rape experience with me in therapy, it had been years since it actually had happened. It was not reported since in the state of Nebraska, the survivor gets to decide herself if she wants to report. She did not. I was following her lead and respected her rights. I wondered throughout my work with her, however, if legal action against any of her perpetrators would have lessened her extreme sense of shame, self-blame, and anger at herself. She would have nothing to do with it.

I concluded my story to my mother, finally deciding to tell her because I didn't know how else to explain my professor's concern. Of course, that day in the car, I did not relate all the details to my mother. But upon hearing the "R" word (rape), she cried. I felt terrible. I knew I hadn't fought hard enough. I'd given in and given up. At that moment, I felt just as I had at the time of the rape: filthy, terrible, miserable. I'd hurt my mother again. What kind of girl was I, anyway?

I had trouble concentrating on the wedding and what I was supposed to do. Ironic—a wedding, the meeting of two beautiful souls who, I was sure, were chaste, pure, and happy—things that were impossible for me to conceive, impossible to be.

Not only does Geri internalize the message that it is all her fault, but also her mother cries and seems to remain silent. This feeds the belief Geri has that she needs to take care of her mother. It confirms what she believed all along, that she is truly a filthy and terrible person. How tragic and how poignant the contrast for Geri as she witnesses the "chaste and pure" wedding, further anchoring her belief that she is undeserving.

It's common for untreated abuse victims such as Geri to have a promiscuous history, primarily because of the belief that they deserve abuse since they are "bad" anyway. Abuse victims are accustomed to not having a voice and to being controlled by the perpetrator. Boundaries are nearly impossible to set and maintain when this is the embedded belief system. The shame victims feel compounds, creating a vicious cycle—one that is often very difficult to break.

7

My Siblings, My Mother

At lunch one day, my sister Lily asked me about this book. I told her that it was going fairly well and that she might be interested to know the role she plays in the narrative. I told her that I thought I understood why she gets so emotional when she thinks about my father's harsh treatment of me. Lily has such a tender heart. The punishments that were meted out to me rarely made sense to her and made her cry. When I mentioned this, her eyes filled with tears.

I appreciate Geri's words regarding this conversation with her sister because it shows so well how the entire family system is wounded by abuse. Just imagine the sister witnessing abuse that made no sense to her and the despair she must have felt in the inability to help her big sister whom she so loved.

I keep wondering why the punishment I received upset Lily so. If it is because she was never sure when or why she might fall under the axe, I can understand. If it was because of knowing how difficult it is to watch your sister being whipped, I can understand that, too. It might also be because we've been very close, sometimes like mother and daughter in the way we've related to each other. Whatever it was it was clearly traumatizing. I wonder if she'll ever get over being sad about it.

Lily has never sought professional help, but she has a wonderful, supportive husband and three marvelous children. She has suffered from depression at times but has never been medicated for it, partly because it is related to hormone issues and partly because she has not always had health insurance. She seems to be doing very well these days, enjoying this phase of life among children and beautiful grandchildren. Like Andrew and me, her faith is very strong, and her trust in God is the most important thing she'd want others to know about her.

Our brother, Andrew, has always been a tough cookie. Yet, he was also deeply affected by the dysfunctional family we all experienced in one way or another. His relationships have been fraught with the tension of nondisclosure, fear, and other things I cannot name. While he has been tacitly supportive, he cannot speak about it. This has created a sense of continued blame and lack of understanding. I so wish it were not so!

I've never been fully able to figure out what my siblings' hurts were and how they have been affected by what happened—what they saw, what they experienced, but I am sorry, so very sorry for their pain. To say that I protected them, or tried to, does not deny that they suffered physically under my father's strict punishments. It seemed almost more difficult to know they were being hurt than to be hurting myself. To be honest I am sometimes envious of my siblings. They seem so settled—emotionally, financially, relationally—so happy now. I have to admit that I sometimes wonder what that feels like. My life has taken a very different path. Very different.

Yes, Geri's siblings now have stable lives due to many of their own resources and also in large part because of Geri' sacrifices. Geri took the hit and protected her siblings. She remembers consciously drawing fire. When she saw her father was irritable, she would find ways to be the target of his anger. Her siblings often blamed her for creating more family tension. She kept the family secret by acting as if all was well, especially in public. She did not want to cause problems for her mother or her siblings. One can argue, and I personally believe that, she kept the secret far too long. Though it seems to have enabled her siblings to live life as if things were "okay" despite their clear observation of the physical abuse. We will never know how much their father could have abused them sexually if Geri had refused him.

Through Geri's process in healing, her relationships with her siblings have grown in honesty and transparency. Her siblings have believed her, number one. Second, they have shown care, support, and compassion. They also seem to truly enjoy each other and have fun together. It's even more important that they all easily come together over the care of their elderly mother.

Recently Mother had a series of illnesses resulting in overall weakness and a difficult recovery period. At 91, she will clearly find a long-term recovery impossible. Aging is the process of losing, bit by bit, abilities to move and to think, and finding fewer and fewer things that are enjoyable. This last period of illness seemed to me more serious than ever. When I offered to return to the States for a brief week's break, my siblings gladly accepted.

As soon as I was able, I arrived at Mother's side and spent several hours with her every day, sharing a meal and time with her. In a way, I may have worn her out! On the other hand, that kind of time together was really quite wonderful. We talked, we laughed, and we really enjoyed each other's company. In spending this kind of time together, I was able to see how I might be helpful to her and how I might be able to alert the nursing staff to her needs. It was a time I will always remember as being one of closeness and shared fun.

Who would have thought that Mother and I would have such an easy time together? I could never have imagined it, and yet, it seems so right, so natural. I discussed this with Seanne and only then realized what a gift this is for both of us. To be able to love and be with my mother without any of the baggage that used to fill the space between us means we now have a kind of wonderful ease with each other that even my brother and sister have noticed. I want to give her a sense of the care and love but especially a sense of the safety she created for me. Writing that now seems a bit foolish because, after all, I wasn't really safe, but I always felt that as long as she was around, I could not, would not die from the things that so scared me.

I can only imagine how different Geri's presence with her mother in this last stage of life would have been had the elephant still been in the room. My experience in other cases is that there is not true emotional intimacy in relationships when any secret exists between the parties, and there often is a cutoff in relationships where no communication at all occurs if issues have not been addressed. The fact that Geri took the risk to openly discuss her abuse with her mother paved the way for her to now be totally emotionally, spiritually, and physically present with her in a very sensitive, compassionate way. Because of the openness in their relationship, the process of forgiveness has also been more complete. As Geri says, there is no excess baggage taking up space between them. They both know; they both grieve the abuse; and they both now love each other through it. They can truly be with each other during this precious and sacred time of her mother's final life stage, which I believe will enable a more peaceful death for her mother.

8

Carol

I first met Carol, a distant relative, when she arrived at the college I was attending. Even though our fathers were related, I had not known her before. She was withdrawn, quiet, and didn't have many friends from what I could see. Her sister, Mary, was also attending the same school but, unlike Carol, she was outgoing and everyone's favorite friend. The comparison between the two could not have been more different. While Mary thrived, Carol didn't last long in college. Within the first semester, she became horribly depressed and unable to attend classes. I suggested she go home. Carol refused to go home, but I couldn't see how she could continue to stay at school. She was on a scholarship and would lose it very quickly under these circumstances. So, I asked her if she wanted to live with my parents for a while. She said she would, and they said she could come.

Really? Geri suggested she live with her parents, thinking they would be able to offer safe refuge? On some level I'm sure they were able to, but Geri suggesting it shows how deeply she had pushed down her own experience. This speaks to the level of Geri's defense mechanisms that served to protect her but kept her in denial.

While staying with my parents, Carol revealed to them that she had been sexually abused by her father. I don't know much about what she shared with my parents as I wasn't around often. However, I do know that

Carol developed a very close relationship with them and always looked to them whenever she had trouble throughout her adult life. I later found out that for Mother, the growing awareness of sexual abuse as described by Carol (and later by young women Mother came in contact with as a minister's wife) was very painful. I will never know how it affected my father.

Of course, Geri did not know the nature of Carol's problems at the time she suggested Carol live with her parents, but it's interesting that Carol herself had an abuse history and fascinating that Carol chose to disclose this secret to Geri's parents. It must have been highly conflicting for Geri's mother to be put in the position of helping Carol.

For a long time, Mother used to quote Carol to us until my sister told her to stop. It seemed to Lily that our parents had showered love and attention on Carol—love and attention that we had missed. I didn't care nor did I want any more attention, but it bothered both my siblings that everything was about how much Carol loved our parents and how great she thought they were. I suppose it helped for Mother and Father to know for certain, and often, that someone did think good things about their parenting skills.

Did I do the right thing in sending her to my parents? Who knows? In hindsight, it sounds like the worst idea possible. It was certainly true that she couldn't return home. I, myself, spent almost all four years at college without returning home except for some Christmas breaks. I did not think about it very much. I just couldn't get home. It was always financially impossible, or so I thought.

The truth is, Geri avoided going home. When she says she "did not think about it much" and that she thought visits were "financially impossible," she was doing a great job at rationalizing her avoidance. Her well-honed denial system perpetuated her avoidant pattern.

After my father's funeral several years ago, Carol's sister (the only one from that side of the family to attend) asked if she could take me out to dinner. It turns out that Mary had figured out from a strange conversation we'd had years ago that my father had done the same thing to me. She wanted to know how I'd dealt with it, what I'd done to get better.

This is a great example why "family secrets" don't work. Someone, somewhere in the generational line, puts two and two together. Of course, the main reason family secrets don't work is that it perpetuates the cycle before someone in the family figures it out. When I work with perpetrators of sex-

ual abuse, I explore with them when, where, and who first sexually abused them. It is highly unlikely that her father or his relative sought help to deal with whatever inappropriate behavior they were exposed to or experienced. Instead, they kept the secret and became perpetrators. It is important, though, to clarify that not all individuals, male or female, who have experienced sexual abuse go on to become perpetrators. Many, like Geri, do not.

Perhaps Mary was hoping to find some way to help Carol as things have been so difficult for her. When Carol tried to tell her family about the sexual abuse from her father, Mary was the only one to believe her. Even though her patience has been tried by Carol's bizarre behaviors and extreme neediness, Mary has continued to support her. Their mother and brother, on the other hand, have refused to believe her. Instead, they have labeled Carol as "a problem" and as "mentally ill" and, ultimately, have seemed to abandon her.

Unfortunately, Mary's support was not enough for Carol, and she turned to self-medicating for relief. Because of her work in the medical field, she has had access to medications that have affected her thinking perhaps as much as the abuse could have. Sadly, she was recently hospitalized after ingesting a toxic mix of self-medications that destroyed her ability to function, at least in the short term.

Recently, I had a long visit with my mother, and she tried to figure out the difference between Carol and me. It made me realize how very grateful I am for the support of my own family. What a huge difference that can make, and maybe that *is* the difference along with finding the right kind of help.

Carol's story is a sad commentary and unfortunately describes what happens all too often when a victim is not heard, not believed, or does not receive intervention. Even though Geri's parents and Mary heard and believed Carol, they did not assist her in finding a mental health professional. So, it appears Carol's shame was internalized and showed itself in self-sabotaging behaviors.

My second therapist is the one who decided that my siblings should be told. Even now, years later, it is difficult for me to imagine the process of telling them. But when I asked Mother if she approved, she said, "Your father and I will be gone someday, but you'll have your brother and sister around a long time, so don't worry about us. Tell them."

Geri is also fortunate that her mother took this position. This attitude is not always the case with mothers of incest victims.

Both my siblings believed me, though, upon hearing it the first time, Lily immediately began crying. Fortunately, her husband was there to comfort her and support her.

While the power of being believed and supported by family members cannot be overstated, and in many cases, support from the family is key, the healing process can occur without literal family involvement. If it is not feasible to have actual family members in sessions or if families are incapable of providing support, I do other interventions such as Internal Family Systems[3] work with clients. This involves using therapy to build up internal ego states so that the client can begin to reparent themselves.

I must say that when Seanne suggested "reparenting" myself, I was resistant. It seemed to me that it was probably useless to try—too late, too difficult, and, bottom line, too hard to change places within myself to become somehow loving, supportive, and encouraging. Ugh! I also resented the idea that somehow I'd have to work harder to make up for missing bits that were not my fault. Ultimately, it was just too hard to believe I deserved a loving parent. It seemed easier to try to avoid this step.

I had to keep underscoring with Geri that yes, it is unfair that she had to work harder, but what were her choices? She could either do the work and become a survivor of incest or live a harder life full of symptoms.

I guess I've been really fortunate in many ways, being able to come out on the other side of this story and live a pretty normal life. I've had advantages in education, friends, and counseling, as well as two siblings and a mother who believed me. I've heard stories like Carol's about young women who are not believed, who find themselves isolated in their own stories, at times wondering whether or not they are true and, subsequently, whether or not they have lost their minds.

It's very healthy Geri can recognize her good fortune, despite how hard her life has been. She has truly moved forward in a way that seems solid.

---

3   This concept is Jungian based but most recently developed by Richard C. Schwartz, Ph.D. His book, *Internal Family Systems Therapy*, discusses working with individuals as systems, working with the understanding that each of us has parts and a Self. The goal of this work is to get the client's parts to get along with one another and help the client's Self.

This is undoubtedly thanks to multiple factors, many that Geri mentions here.

9

I Don't Belong to Myself

When I started this project, I promised myself I'd be honest, but what I have to tell next is embarrassing and humiliating. It is difficult not to feel guilt and personal responsibility for the sexual relationships and casual meetings that seemed to keep occurring over and over.

A significant factor in Geri's healing process is her decision (finally) to be honest. I applaud her strength and courage in doing so.

Breakfast with Philip this morning, a long-time friend from grad school, reminded me of the challenge it is for me to write about this part of the story. He wasn't just a friend. He was the longest and last chapter in a whole book of chapters, some of them very short—one night—and others a bit longer. I wouldn't call Philip a lover because I had no real love for him, but he was the last casual partner I allowed into my life.

It was after the rape incident that I began to accept the fact that I had no other value than sexual, at least to men. It became clear to me that if men asked, I would say yes without thinking. It wasn't that I wanted to say yes. I didn't believe I had the right to say no. I always felt a kind of sickening dread in my stomach that saying yes, while scary, was inevitable. It became a long, miserable pattern and confirmed again and again that I was amoral and wicked—just like my father had said I was. Part of that pattern may have been cultural, too, because where we lived, women really had few rights. However, I had been brought up to understand what "nice" girls did and did not do. I was not a nice girl.

This is a huge dynamic that plays out over and over when sexual abuse has occurred. This is especially common when the abuse starts at an early age, is progressive in frequency and violation, and is sustained over time. Obviously, it is compounded by the secrecy factor. The victim of abuse loses her sense of self. She literally has no voice. As Geri says, she didn't want to say yes, but there was not the strength of core self to assertively say no. She truly had the sense she didn't own her own body, so she didn't feel she had the right to say no since, in her mind, her body didn't belong to her. It set up the self-fulfilling prophecy in her belief system that she was indeed "amoral and wicked." When she believed that, consequences followed. She felt she had no value other than as a sexual object. Sexual abuse frequently makes victims feel like "damaged goods," which often leads to either promiscuity or the acceptance of multiple sexual partners as inevitable.

There were a few times I tried to get help. I remember one incident after I had been released from the hospital the first time. I had been dragged there by friends and a therapist who'd determined I was suicidal. Some weeks after my release, I was asked to pick up a visiting pianist from the airport. I was to invite Robert to dinner and get him to his hotel. At dinner, he began to drink, ordering bottle after bottle of Soave Bolla. Since even one glass of wine gives me migraines, I was taking the smallest of sips. Robert soon began reaching under the table for my legs. I became alarmed and excused myself to use the pay phone. I called my therapist, but his wife said he was ill and couldn't come to the phone. I hung up the phone and walked slowly back to the table, knowing that I was in trouble. A kind of weariness came over me, a hopelessness and a sense that I already knew how the evening would end.

When we got to the hotel, it was clear to me that he could not make it up to his room on his own. There were no bellboys to help. As a matter of fact, there are no bellboys in our whole rural town. I grabbed his suit hanger and arm while he tried to manage a small suitcase, and we rode the elevator to the fifth floor. I unlocked the door and pushed him in. Then, stepping in myself, I hung up his suit and turned to leave. But I couldn't leave. He blocked the door, grabbed me, and pushed me over on the bed two steps away. He began pulling my clothes off. I don't remember exactly what happened after that, or how it was that he raped me, but I'm sure that

I did not fight back much. I just know that, as usual, I was numb, physically and emotionally.

When I got back to the lobby, I called a friend who asked me if I wanted to go to the hospital. I said no and went home. After I'd showered and felt a bit more settled, I called my friend again. She asked me again if I wanted to go to the hospital. I didn't. What would I say? How could I say that I "let someone rape me?" I mean, that doesn't sound like rape, does it? No, I would hope and pray I wasn't pregnant and try to pretend that everything was okay. I felt separated from a body that I could not seem to protect. What was wrong with me, I asked myself for the millionth time?

The compounding shame from traumatic experiences becomes highly toxic and feeds the paralysis that perpetuates the cycle.

The next day, I told a close friend (a member on the Arts Board) what had happened and made her promise not to leave me that night until Robert was safely in his hotel room. As we walked down the aisle to our seats for his concert that night, I said, "Well, I could rate his performance right now, before he ever plays a note!" I thought my friend was going to collapse on the spot! Of course, it wasn't true. I had no idea about his "performance." As usual, I hadn't remembered anything except realizing I had to get my clothes back on.

Later that week, in therapy, my crazy therapist was elated. This, apparently, was exactly what he'd hoped for. Huh? Somehow, he saw this rape as therapeutic. I tried to see this as the happy event he did, but it felt all wrong to me. Instead, I just felt more miserable and petrified for the next time. I couldn't convince him that what I wanted, what I needed, were ways to ensure I was safe, ways to tell the next person "No," so that it could not be mistaken for anything else.

That same therapist, Mark, had obliquely mentioned that he could arrange for me to "meet someone" in a hotel sometime. I always pretended that I didn't know what he was talking about. Like my father who was showing me "love," this man said he was going to help me by using sex.

Her therapist's inappropriate and incompetent response is inexcusable. Harm was done by this therapist. This therapist's license to practice had already been terminated, and he had moved from the state by the time Geri came to me. Otherwise, I would have reported him to the state licensure board. It is tragic that some therapists do not know how to define "harm". Unfortunately, some therapists have their own unmet needs and use clients as a way of meeting them. There were not many therapeutic choices in our community when Geri first began therapy. Additionally, vulnerable clients have a much harder time being assertive with authority figures so are more likely to fall prey to predator type therapists.

Yes, there were next times. It began to matter less and less. At least, that's what I told myself. I imagined that since I didn't really believe I had the rights to myself, it didn't matter what anyone wanted or did. I believed that I was stumbling through the world with Hawthorne's scarlet letter on my forehead. There had to be a reason for the numerous encounters that eventually included women, too. I was so confused, sometimes wondering if I were a lesbian or just so separated from myself that I would never learn who I really was.

As I said, Philip was the last one. I would like to think that he was the last because I learned what I needed to learn—that I do have the right to my own body and I *can* say no. But, I'm not really sure about that. I do know that during this time, my spiritual development, my sense of God in my life, and my commitment to maintaining that sense of His presence was a source of great strength to me.

Geri's spiritual development is a helpful resource and another signifi-cant factor in her ability to heal. I think this is true on a number of levels, one being that she began experiencing redemption for the first time in her life because of the reassurances of her pastor and friends over time. She had the desire to know God, and she seemed to feel deserving of His presence. This strengthened her in assertively using her voice.

When I told Philip I couldn't handle the dichotomy of what I believed to be true for me morally with what I was doing, he said he understood.

This was clearly a positive move for Geri, and, thank God, Philip didn't push it.

I guess I had always felt obliged to have sex with him because, some-how, I felt he deserved this "payment" from me for not always pulling my weight in the translation exercise we were doing together for a graduate class.

The whole issue of belonging to myself felt like a puzzle that couldn't be put back together because I kept trying to give away, again and again, the same pieces my father stole.

10

Sweet Sleep

I was visiting a friend from college last week. Even in college I knew her to be a girl who needed at least nine hours of sleep each night. When I first discovered this, I was shocked. Who could stand to be in bed that much? Then, on a Sunday morning show, the designer Diane von Furstenberg showed off her bed designs with the statement, "Everything important happens in bed. What could be more important than your bed?"

I was suddenly angry, but I realized it's all too true. Everything important—even bad everythings—happen in bed. Shakespeare wrote:

> Sleep that knits up the raveled sleave of care
> The death of each day's life, sore labour's bath
> Balm of hurt minds, great nature's second course,
> Chief nourisher in life's feast.

> - Act II, Sc. II, *Macbeth*.

The first time I read this, it resonated with me so powerfully that I never forgot it. It seemed to be so true and, even though it sounded like a fantasy, I really liked the sound of it. Of course, Macbeth is referring to the murder he's committed that has "murdered sleep." Incest isn't murder, but sometimes I wished it had been.

So, when my friends talk about how much they enjoy sleeping, going to bed, sleeping in, or snuggling under the covers, I shudder. I wonder if I'll ever get used to the idea of "sweet sleep." Probably not. Rather, when I hear things like that I become irritated and sometimes anxious. People sending me emails detailing how sleep improves brain function, increases metabolic speed, and even lengthens life only increases my anxiety. At times, I'm sure I appear stubborn, appearing to refuse the "help" people want to send my way. But I do appreciate the advice. I am willing to try to create new habits and patterns. So far, though, my tendency is to stay up, find a myriad of things to do, and then awaken early and unhappy. The longer I stay in bed, the unhappier I am. Getting up is the best way to clear my head and the best way to begin to feel more normal before the day begins.

At one point during therapy, I began to have increasingly more trouble getting into bed when I was finally ready. I suppose it was a time when we were talking about difficult things. I don't remember. But every time I got into bed, I found myself crying for a long time before dropping off to sleep hours later.

I became increasingly depressed, and one night I called my minister. He and his wife came over; both have counseling backgrounds. I like their practical approach to problem solving. She said, "Well then, just don't go to bed. Fall asleep here, on the sofa." It was months before I finally went back to my bed with some sleep restored at last.

This is helpful feedback for me because I know I have not always been cognizant of the residual impact of therapy sessions. Would I have opted not to "talk about difficult things," knowing Geri was being set up for sleepless nights? Would that mean I wasn't really doing my job? Did I adequately check in and help Geri with "containment skills" at the closure of sessions that were particularly difficult for her? Did I encourage Geri to call me if she was having difficulty with emotional self-regulation post session? (There is always a fine line in not wanting to create dependency on the therapist, yet to be available for the client when truly needed.) I honestly don't remember, but I can't say with certainty that I did all the right things. It's been many years since I was Geri's therapist. Did I even inquire deeply enough how she was sleeping? Did she voluntarily offer that information? I can't say for sure. I am grateful that she called upon her good friends who offered skilled assistance.

(I remember calling Seanne at particularly difficult times, but usually, I was careful not to take advantage of her non-working hours. I remember that when I did finally decide to pick up the phone, I could hardly breathe. I always expected Seanne to be impatient with after-hours calls. She never was, but I never got over my fear.)

The role of therapist is a very humbling one. Even with good intentions, we do not always do all that needs to be done. We cannot really know the response of clients when they leave our office. Even with the best "checking in," we can't really know how a client is interpreting or processing the therapy. One hopes to teach the skills of emotional self-regulation that the client can utilize between sessions. However, the client is frequently not really ready to learn these skills because they are already overwhelmed, making the client less than receptive to new information. Thankfully, Geri had the desire to master what she could. It just takes time.

I've learned a number of things about the phenomenon of sleep, and I realize that it probably isn't really a "phenomenon" to others. Early morning fussing, for me around 3:30 or so, is best dealt with by getting up fully and then returning to bed sitting up. If I prop myself up with mountains of pillows I feel somehow calmer, even positive again, so I can return to sleep—eventually. There are times when I am able to lie down again before morning. More often, however, I find myself still sitting up with a sore back when the alarm goes off. Learning how to manage this has taken a long time (more than 40 years), and my friends would love to think that the need for such tactics has disappeared altogether. I wonder if it ever will.

A number of years ago, I discovered that I, along with millions of others, hated to go to the dentist. I wondered, what was really going on? These days, dentistry is not painful. It certainly wasn't painful at my dentist's, but I put off going for years.

Finally, during intense sessions of therapy, I made a connection that has allowed me to keep my teeth in good repair ever since. I discovered that when I'm tipped back in the chair and look up to see a man standing over me, my breathing becomes shallow. I find my hands grip the chair, my voice deserts me, and tears start to come to my eyes—all this before the dentist has even touched my mouth. It would probably have been evident to anyone else that there was much more going on here (emotionally speaking) than a simple dental appointment, but I was always too petrified to think it through properly.

I'm not sure when the epiphany happened, but when it did, I let the dentist know. Or rather, I asked a friend to do that. Immediately, things began to change for me. My dentist was careful never to leave his chair in a reclining position. He would tip it back when he worked and immediately return it to an upright position as soon as he was finished or had to leave the room. He was particularly careful to "check in" with me frequently. "How are you doing?" "Are you OK?" he would ask.

Now, I have very little anxiety when I go. I think it is not only that he checks in or tips the chair up. That has helped. It is also that, in his sensitivity, he lowers his voice and moves more slowly. I always know where he is, what he's doing, and what he's going to do.

This was a breakthrough in therapy when Geri could consciously choose to enter her adult self by getting out of the child self (who had no voice). She had already carefully chosen a dentist with high compassion and empathy, whom she basically trusted. I emphasized this fact to her frequently. Even though she cognitively knew he was trustworthy, her body had its own automatic response. I encouraged her to allow her good friend to help with the dentist issue. She gave me permission to coach her friend on how to communicate Geri's issues with the dentist. Her friend was highly skilled and effective with this intervention. The process of communication with the dentist went well and gave Geri an experience of mastery, thus reinforcing and building the adult self-ego strength.

Of course, the dentist is just one in a long list of things I gradually discovered were problems for me as a result of my father's nightly visits to my room. I cannot say when these visits began, but I do have clear memories of incidents of sexual and physical abuse at age 4.

When I say "clear memories," that hardly describes the clarity and power of remembering. I had already been in therapy for several years and was seeing Pamela at the time. Standing at the kitchen sink, I was washing dishes, when all of a sudden I couldn't breathe. I stood very still because the picture of my father and me at the beach was as clear as crystal. He held me on his knee with one hand, below water level, while with the other, he pulled my swimsuit aside and reached up and in with his finger. I remember squirming, but he was too strong. He seemed to be practiced, confident; he knew exactly what he was doing. The physical sensation of the memory couldn't be ignored. I felt it and knew it was true.

We will never know when the actual first incident of sexual abuse occurred with Geri, or how old she was. Fondling and digital penetration could have begun as early as her infant years. The fact that she remembers her father's "practiced" abusive actions makes me wonder. We do know he targeted her at a very young age. Memory is an interesting phenomenon. While Geri may have been pre-verbal when the abuse began, her body remembered. And her body viscerally remembered in her adult life, after she had begun therapy. The flashback was so strong and clear that even today she remembers where she was standing when the memory washed over her as she says, with clarity and power.

My mother tells me that the physical abuse began while I was still in diapers, before I was two. Some time, and for sure by age 9, my father began coming into my bedroom very early in the morning. I've read many stories about child-victims feigning sleep. I think that this reveals every child-victim's need to hope, pretend, and even believe that what was happening really wasn't. Were his hands reaching under my nightdress? Rubbing my tiny breasts? Were his hands pushing my legs apart? His fingers pushing up and rubbing the sensitive area that shocked me at first? Was that really his voice I heard; the voice that seemed to be so scary in the night? His voice took on a completely different sound; a sound that seemed more menacing than even his angry voice. And how could he refer to his own body part, a disgusting, hard something protruding from his pajama shorts as "he"? "He wants you to touch him; he wants you to squeeze him, hard." Somehow, this (touching him) was much, much more difficult than being the passive recipient. Then there was no pretending that I hadn't been an active participant. There was no pretending I was still asleep and no pretense that I wasn't complicit in what was going on. Even now, as I write about this, I cannot be completely objective. It is difficult to breathe properly, and I find that observing all this, even from this distance, requires this bit of "taking stock" of my emotions and "checking with myself" as another, later therapist would say.

This describes well the insidious nature of abuse. It is progressive and usually well calculated by the perpetrator. They prepare the victim for the incremental steps of more and more invasive abuse by checking their control over the victim and assessing the likelihood of sustained secrecy. So, what started with fondling obviously kept progressing. Geri understandably pretended to be asleep, but then was forced to be a participant, perpetuating her sense of shame.

During those years, I often wondered if I could sleep on my stomach and hang on to the bed. Then, maybe he wouldn't be able to reach me. Though I was awake by the time he got to the bed, I tried desperately to pretend sleep. Yet, the moment he opened the door, I was instantly alert. Being forcibly turned over on my back made it impossible to believe that I could have fooled him or myself that I was still asleep. Then the layers of pretending grew deeper. I started pretending that I was pretending to believe I was still asleep. Next, I began to develop my abilities in taking myself away and simply not being there anymore. I would feel myself float to the top corner of the ceiling and look down on the child, the child who disgusted me more and more with each incident of verbal, physical, or sexual abuse. The real "me" was stuck in her body, and it was not fair! She was the one who was causing all this; she was the one I wanted to get rid of. If she weren't there, I could be happy.

This was the beginning of Geri's dissociative pattern. While dissociating served Geri at the time, it went on to have rather severe, adverse effects in her life. After much therapy and intentional effort on Geri's part, she can now manage her dissociative behavior rather than letting it manage her. Her split of self (the "good-girl" and the "bad-girl"), however, created an internal dichotomy that even today feeds suicidal ideation.

Despite my best efforts to leave my body I was not so dissociated that I could not feel orgasms. The fact that my father sensed them and was pleased by them, (making his breathing heavier on my face, his movements between my legs more frantic) caused me to hate them. I did everything I could to delay their apparent inevitability and to quiet the telltale shudders he liked to feel. Even my doctor's reassurance, many years later, that the sexual responses I felt were impossible to totally control, did not relieve my guilt in responding to the man I hated nor did it stop me from hating my body for betraying me.

It took a long time before my father eventually got in bed and climbed on top of me. I still do not remember what happened next but by then, his fingers had already been to places I had not known before.

We spent long therapy hours dealing with the shame that was caused by Geri's automatic sexual responses. I'm not sure it is possible to completely eradicate shame when there are so many layers supporting it. A more realistic goal is to acquire tools to manage it, catching it early with keen awareness of when it is the operating core emotion.

Later, I would get up very, very early, before any alarm and dress immediately for school. I would try to sit at my desk and study and wait for morning. This seemed to create a barrier my father would not cross. It seems he could not ask me to undress, and I must have known that on some level. Once I developed this tactic, I tried hard to get up whenever I awoke. The problem was that out of a sense of duty, or perhaps guilt, I was also staying up late with my mother who worked into the night in the home office we had. I did not want her to have to stay up alone so late at night. Not surprisingly, I developed strange sleep habits that have been difficult to break.

When I was around fifteen, nightly visits finally stopped, wrapped in lies and deceit. I will never, ever forget that day. It should have been a happy day, but Father's "confession" to Mother was different from the "confession" he made to me. What he told me still embarrasses me today. He asked that I lie on the bed, naked. He promised he would come in and demonstrate that he would not touch me. Because now I knew he had told Mother, I refused. Because he had told, he appeared weaker and vulnerable. I felt I had the advantage. Besides, he had hurt my mother, making me so angry at him that it became one of the most difficult things to forgive.

Geri Henderson & Seanne Emerton

11

Salvation in School

A couple of years ago, while completing my second year teaching at a university overseas, I became increasingly frustrated and upset by the circumstances of the classroom and of everything else connected with my position there—students who didn't care and an administration that had difficulty respecting and listening to the wishes or even the deepest concerns of faculty. Our positions and the respect we could usually expect were continually undercut by decisions of the previous dean or chair who often sided with students. We were crowded in pairs into dirty, cave-like offices that hadn't been updated in decades. I immediately began looking for another position. Immediately. But it proved very difficult and, at my age, I really could not expect much other than an administrative position somewhere. All of a sudden, my anger at being deceived, ignored, and betrayed turned into something else entirely.

I began to think about all the time and energy I have spent just maintaining my life, just trying to stay alive. I have lost decades to survival. Unlike my friends who settled into productive and satisfying careers and arrived at the completions of their life's work and fulfilling retirements, I found myself still trying to find that one position that will work for me long-term, something that will take me up through my final years of work. I realized too, that all the years I'd spent in school had been years needing something to occupy my mind and energy, years when I couldn't be still, couldn't find peace, and was never happy. Maybe it's not possible for me to live or work anywhere happily. Could it be that more, much more, than my childhood was robbed and that now I cannot feel settled, happy, or even content? Perhaps, I'm being overdramatic, but sometimes I resent all the time it has taken me just to survive, to find my way.

Of course, all these years and years in school, in different jobs, and in therapy kept me poor, exhausted, and worried most of the time. I wonder if it was easier to be worried about money and time than it was to be honest about the tigers that chased me.

I have been told, even recently, that I'm an intellectual, an academic. That's good—I do see myself as a teacher, someone who likes to learn, someone who enjoys research, writing, and thinking. But, also recently, I was asked whether or not I thought the reason I had buried myself in school and university studies for most of my life was that I was trying to hide or distract my mind from things that were truly painful. I think that would be nearly impossible to know for sure, but it might be partly right.

I remember that studies and music practice (piano, violin, and guitar) were safe activities where I was usually left in peace. I had always planned to get a terminal degree. I thought I'd never be happy without it and that I would certainly be happy when I "finished" my education. I am not so sure now. What was a refuge turned into an albatross at times—a burden that I was determined to carry across the finish line, no matter what. Most PhD students would say that, I think. The cost has been great. I *think* I am happier with what I believe to be a "finished" education, but I am not sure. The "doing" of it was always exciting, completely engaging, sometimes frightening, and sometimes overwhelming, but I believe I would have done it even had I known what was ahead.

My Master of Music degree took 12 long and painful years, and when it was all over, I felt stupid and inadequate. I'd worked most of that time with the same professor in piano, including for my thesis. As a piano teacher, he was very, very helpful, and I learned things I could directly apply to my teaching and performance. However, as a thesis advisor, he was quite different. His demands were often inscrutable, at least to me. I would revise a chapter exactly according to his additions and suggestions only to find out the next week that it was unacceptable. He was brutal and expected me to be assertive and argue with him. I couldn't. He was an authority figure who completely intimidated me, and so I often cried for over an hour, all the way home.

What was worse though, was that my first therapist had told my professor why I'd missed lessons (I was hospitalized). This information seemed to give him another "in" to my personal life. He used to try to get me to discuss it or align himself with me, condemning my father completely. He would say, "Either you love your daughter completely and could never do those things to her or you hate her."

This is an example of an ethical violation that is inexcusable. Geri had not signed a release of information nor given verbal permission for this therapist to contact her piano professor. This piece of information enabled him to abuse his power even more with Geri.

One Friday afternoon I received a call from the music office telling me that my professor had suffered a severe heart attack and had been admitted to the hospital. My lessons and meetings with him were cancelled until further notice. Despite the misery he'd put me through, I was devastated and wondered how on earth I'd finish. Actually, the result was that I finished even faster because of my professor's heart attack. I heard from friends that they thought he "had something for me," a fact I could hardly believe. Sadly, I later found it was true, but it must have been a very selfish "something" since he did all he could to delay completion of my thesis and graduation.

In his absence, the chair of the department looked over my thesis and declared, "You've finished. Dr. Fields will be out of the hospital in time to sit in on your oral defense."

By that time, I was so tired and so disgusted with the whole process, that I requested my diploma be mailed to me. When people attempted to congratulate me, I could hardly appreciate it. Instead, I said, "Anyone else, more intelligent, would have finished earlier or known when to quit."

The last time I saw Dr. Fields was at coffee sometime after graduation. He told me that we could not meet again. When I asked why not? He said, "You are the problem." Really? Since my friends had told me they thought the reason I would never finish was because he liked me too much and inappropriately, it began to make sense even though I hadn't believed them. While I did not miss him, I did think about the strangeness of the final meeting. Upon hearing of my plans to pursue a Ph.D. in English, Dr. Fields tried to discourage me, telling me that most people never finish. Besides, his constant haranguing had destroyed my confidence as a writer.

After attending my first English graduate classes, I took myself to the Writing Center for the help I was convinced I needed. The grad student assigned to me gave me a couple of writing prompts and 30 minutes later, puzzled, asked, "Why are you here?"

I replied, "Because my Master of Music advisor said I don't know how to write." His eyes got big, "Huh?"

I never went back. Having taken only one English course for my undergraduate degree, I was told I needed to qualify for graduate entrance to the MA program in English. So, I took graduate courses that would apply to the MA requirements and hoped it would lead to a PhD.

Dr. Fields was another male in Geri's world who was abusing the power in the relationship. It's as if she set herself up for this, unintentionally of course. This dysfunctional dynamic felt normal to her. Her boundaries were poor, and she felt she had no right to stand up for herself. So, she presented herself with passive acceptance at the hands of this male who abused power and control.

Working full-time, volunteering in my community, and then adding an additional full-time position at another university campus, more than filled my time. I took a long time to finish all these degrees. Over the years, this limited the amount of time I could spend thinking about the issues brought up in therapy. True, there were times I was absolutely paralyzed by what I was forced to think about, and other times I was so deeply depressed, I was suicidal. But I kept moving forward, somehow, working as much as I could to pay the bills. I never applied for help because I believed I would never get an assistantship or scholarship. At one point, I lived in two places, 100 miles apart, teaching lessons in the university city to pay for the extra apartment. What strange times those were!

I did finish an MA and a PhD, but by then I could honestly say I had been in school for most of my life, at least 45 years. I am not really sure now what that frenetic pace did for me. I do know that the delay in finishing my degrees was, in large part, because there was so much energy, time, and money going into therapy, and being in and out of the hospital. Also, the long breaks I sometimes took from therapy would force me back to try to put the pieces together again.

By the time I was an age at which I felt ready to face the world, literally, I was beyond being a "fresh, young graduate" looking forward to many years of scholarly contribution. Also, my entree to professional academia was about as far away from my safety net of friends, family, and help as I could have gotten. It has been a very bumpy ride since then. Sometimes, I feel very confident; other times, I wonder why I ever thought I could do what I am trying to do.

One spring semester, being unable to find work closer to friends and family, I began to question everything I'd ever done and the reasons for which I'd done it all. I have thought, "You love music, but that doesn't make you a musician. You love to read and write, but that doesn't make you a scholar." The other nagging thoughts, the painful ones, some that I mentioned before, keep recurring: "If only you hadn't needed to spend so much money, time, and energy in therapy, you'd be well on your way to completing a life's work of which you could be proud. As it is, you're still floundering, still wondering what your contribution might be, and still hoping there might have been something you contributed somewhere you've not remembered. Your siblings have lovely families and happy middle years while you, you're trying to find the place where you'll be satisfied, fulfilled, and happy. Your siblings are worried about *you*, and that was never supposed to be the way things were." It feels very, very wrong.

Though academic life as a professor is very compelling, real life, i.e. the life issues that hit me in the face, interferes far too often. I like to think I might have had a successful and smoother career path without all the emotional garbage I dragged around.

The cost of her childhood and subsequent mental health issues took a toll. She used school both intellectually and emotionally for engagement and distraction. It has taken a very long time for her to attain a professional status that many similarly credentialed professionals, who are younger than she, enjoy. She gained and lost during her schooling. Who knows where Geri would be professionally without her history? She is brilliant and undoubtedly could have been at the top of her game in any chosen profession. The price she has paid is high.

Geri Henderson & Seanne Emerton

12

Physical Abuse and Siblings

I was telling someone about my academic woes. As I said before, it's been a year that made me question everything about who I was (I've always thought of myself as a teacher) and what on earth I thought I'd accomplished by this time in my life. I have felt so useless, and this has led to the other, darker thoughts I mentioned such as, "If only I hadn't had to spend decades just learning how to stay alive, how to cope, how to manage to live in the world..."

Hearing this, my friend replied, "But Geri, remember you took care of your siblings."

That is somewhat true. Most of the time I did what I could to protect them and draw the heat. I remember times, too, that I would say things I knew would be irritating to my father to deflect his attention from them.

Later on, sometime during therapy, I became concerned about this. I went to my minister to ask him about it. "Was it a sin," I asked, "to purposely irritate my father for that reason?"

He replied, "Yes, but a noble sin."

Placing blame seemed to be important to my father. He was never satisfied until he had someone to punish, sometimes severely, for anything he interpreted as bad behavior or even just carelessness. Often, when I heard him begin a sentence with, "Who.....?" I would quickly answer, "I did!"

I discovered early on that hearing my brother or sister being punished was much more painful than being punished myself. Besides, I would think, I probably *was* the one who did whatever father was yelling about. There was one time when Lily had been whipped. I stayed in my room and cried while I heard her cries. Then, I went to her to comfort her, something Father would never allow Mother to do.

When I saw the red marks on her legs, I ran to the bedroom where Father was and screamed at him, "You left *red marks* on her legs!" I remember repeating this several times, in tears, leaving my father so shocked at this bold arrogance that he didn't say anything, nor did he bring it up again. Now, when I think of it, I hardly believe I could have done that.

On some level Geri knew she had power over her father, and she called it in here. The abuser always lives with the fact that the victim indeed has a great deal of power over him (or her) because even though the victim is fear-bound, the abuser always knows the victim could tell the secret at any time. It's not uncommon for this dynamic to be displayed with brazen behavior by the victim. Geri was not brazen but had no real respect for her father, and he had to know that.

I can recall only the specifics of a few beatings. He used his belt, and I was made to undress and bend over the bed. Mother remembers more of them very clearly. She especially remembers the time Lily was in bed for a year with rheumatic fever. My sister was not supposed to get out of bed for any reason. I do remember trying to help, sometimes in tears, seeing her so ill. One time, my help was not to my father's liking, and I was whipped harshly. He left bruises everywhere.

Mother remembers trying to explain that I was only trying to help, but that made my father even angrier. He told her, "Fine then, I'll just stay out of the children's lives, and you can raise them yourself!"

She said that she told him that would be fine. He didn't, of course. Perhaps it was about that time she thought about leaving him but couldn't seem to figure out how to do it. She had no money, couldn't tell anyone, and couldn't imagine what would happen to the churches they were involved in building and establishing.

Geri's empathy for her mother and her mother's position is notable, but again, her high empathy contributed to Geri's tendency to turn her anger inward on herself. I often found myself wondering about how Geri did not seem to feel much, if any, anger toward her mother for not protecting her. Perhaps it's partly because Geri was bright enough to discern the no-win position her mother was in. They lived at a time and in a place where resources for help weren't readily available. The family was economically dependent upon Geri's father, and they were quite isolated. These are common ingredients found in abusive family and organizational systems. Even if resources had been available, there is such a strong, unspoken rule in abusive families not to talk about the elephant in the room that intervention is not easily obtained, at least not voluntarily. There is also a strong, unspoken rule to protect each other (which is why not only family systems but also other systems, such as educational systems, "protect each other" even in the face of obvious abuse by powerful figures.) The power of denial is very strong.

I remember the time my father found little check marks in a book I had. I was reading well by the time I was 5 and had marked the Bible stories I had read—most of them. Father beat me for each one, repeating over and over, "Do *not* write in books. Never write in books." It took me years of re-education to understand that there are, in fact, very good reasons for writing in books. It took me even longer to learn to mark fingerings and notes in my musical scores.

Among the many probable issues in my father's life was the fact that he had had little teaching growing up. He didn't even have table manners, so Mother used the opportunity of teaching us appropriate behavior to teach him too. Despite watching her, he clung to the belief that beatings *were* a teaching method.

Mother has wondered what she might have done had she known the whole story of the sexual abuse. Who knows? I think her position was pretty impossible really, and I have told her so. She says—and she does not believe—that sacrificing a child is right for any reason and yet...

There really are no good answers for second-guesses and hindsight.

It took Geri a long time to break the unspoken family rules and to gather the courage to have honest conversations with her mother and her siblings. Just doing this much can shift the pattern and break the abuse cycle.

One terrible time, my little sister, Lily, was whipped for something I did! She no longer remembers this, but it still makes me sad. Before I knew what had happened, Father had accused her, and her protests only made Father believe she was lying. I told her over and over how sorry I was. From her position, Lily still wonders why Father was so much harder on me than he was on Andrew and her. Who knows? But the recollection of his anger can still reduce Lily to sad silence on my behalf. Lily remembers a time playing with me in the backyard when I stumbled and sprained my ankle badly. Since Mother was not home, Lily had to get Father for help. Instead of an assurance that Father would care for me, she worried about how angry Father would be with me when he was told.

Who knows why Geri was the targeted one? She is the oldest in her sibling strip; her father was the youngest in his. Was it because she was the most like him temperamentally and intellectually? Did she most resemble him or his side of the family? Although we will never fully understand it, for some reason it seems her father projected onto Geri his own, undealt-with "demons." It is a known fact in Geri's family her father was sexually abused by his brothers. He obviously had not done his own work on his issues, perhaps even denying them to himself, setting up the abuse cycle to continue. Thank God, this cycle ended with Geri.

As I write this, I question how well I protected my siblings. Not very well, I decide. I did all I could think to do, but they suffered too, just for different reasons. Part of the reason they suffered was that we were so close and what was meant to hurt me also hurt them. As they became adults they, too, had to deal with depression and other issues related to growing up as we did.

Without a doubt, Geri did all she could to help protect her siblings. I'm sure they were much more protected because of her efforts even though no one is spared in an abusive family system. Even if they weren't the direct recipients of the abuse itself, they were emotionally abused in different ways. Just being in an abusive family takes a huge emotional toll on everyone in the system. There are secrets to keep, and an atmosphere of "don't ask, don't tell" prevails. As Geri said, her siblings have had their own issues to deal with as adults.

As a result of her role in protecting her sister and brother, Geri developed a keen sense of wanting to protect others. This has created its own problems in that she puts others before herself and before her own needs. Doing so creates enabling types of behaviors and has frequently gotten Geri back into a victim stance rather quickly. In the world of emotional intelligence (EI) language, I would say Geri's empathy skills have often been too high in comparison to her low assertiveness skills.

However, as Geri has healed, her assertiveness and her own emotional self-awareness have grown, helping her stay more balanced with this need-

to-protect issue. Her emotional intelligence in general has grown by leaps and bounds through all her therapy and life experiences. Yet, the area of self-regard seems to stay stubbornly low.

Where does reality about one's abilities and limitations end and sink into low self-esteem? I don't think I'll ever know the answer to that. I do know there are some times when I imagine that I'm a good teacher or a good aunt, sister, or friend. But then, I think I'm fooling myself. On the other hand, I don't think I'll ever be able to "accept [myself], warts and all." As a matter of fact, the idea sounds ludicrous.

This is a good example of how we have to choose our battles and prioritize accordingly. I would have lost Geri therapeutically speaking if I would have pressed too hard on the issue of mastering self-regard. As a therapist however, it is hard to accept that "it is what it is" with some things. Of course, Geri finds the concept of truly and fully accepting herself ludicrous. Yet, the fact is that she was able to grow her compassion for self by reducing her shame. This came about in many ways and not just by therapeutic techniques. Her loyalty to friends and family provided her with healthy, reciprocal relationships where she experienced truly being loved. This cannot be underestimated as a huge contributor to her healing process. For those not so fortunate in having positive support systems, it is possible to work with a good therapist who will coach and guide clients in developing the life line that good friends can be.

Yes, it was respect for my friends that forced me to accept some of the things they told me about myself. I couldn't think of them as liars, and they were intelligent. My rational mind said that I had to believe, as best I could, what they said.

Geri has truly wonderful friends, without whom her healing would not have been possible.

13

Body, Mine?

Last spring I had an annual checkup with my doctor. The findings were not good as far as vascular health is concerned. At the same time, Seanne asked me to research "adrenal stress." Two doctors confirmed that continual adrenal stress can result in a number of the physical problems that I'm struggling with, including the dangerous cholesterol/triglyceride levels they saw. There are other things too—allergies that seem to be increasing in number; obesity (also increasing at times); eczema so severe for several years, from ages 7 to 9, that I had to receive injections; and a need for caffeine, almost constantly until bedtime. But there are some things I haven't experienced from adrenal stress, including a suppression of one's auto-immune system. I seem to be almost impervious to germs, rarely having even a cold, never having flu or the other things that seem to force others to bed. The only nagging, chronic problem has been migraines, and those can be connected to so many things, I guess. I used to have debilitating PMS and menstrual pain, but an early hysterectomy eliminated that at age 39.

This bit of writing, though is not related to any of that—or perhaps it is. What it brings up is that a complete denial of my body—a denial that it exists—leads to its deterioration sooner rather than later.

This is a powerful point. The price of abuse is paid on so many levels with body/mind/spirit. Geri has spent most her life neglecting the needs of her body, acting with the idea that if she ignored it, it would go away. The head-in-the-sand approach caught up with her. Luckily, Geri healed enough emotionally to wake up and become aware of the body's needs. She's not always consistent in honoring these needs (who is?), but at least now she is more aware and more intentional in her physical self-care.

It is a strange phenomenon, at least to me, that when I have had some success in healthy lifestyle changes, I can't maintain them for long. I remember a time when I used the Diet Center program to help me lose weight before surgery. It worked well, but at the time I had a housemate who cooked, encouraged, and pushed me to stick with it. After surgery, my weight slowly went back up. The next time I tried to go back to the Diet Center, I was back to living alone and was angry and miserable most of the time. I never did figure out what was going on, but I do know that the more I focus on my physical needs the more I rebel and the more I rebel the more I can hate myself.

Body image and weight issues are common with survivors of incest and sexual abuse. From an early age, Geri seemed to develop a well-honed containment system, so to speak, where she not only dissociated from her body but never wanted to focus on her body because it caused her so much shame. She chose, instead, to focus on her mind, and that seemed to serve her well as a coping strategy at the time. But the body catches up and demands attention either in health-related issues or just in dealing with the nuisance of obesity, for instance. (Some survivors develop eating disorders or become overly sexualized with their body image. Some want extra weight so they are not targeted as sexual objects.) Geri simply has wanted to deny her body by ignoring it. It is a real sign of progress that today, at least, she is paying attention to it with consistent exercise and attention to good nutrition.

Of course, I know that any sane person is probably wondering how I can keep trying to believe that I do not physically take up space in the world, that my body is somehow not here. I've always tried to be a brain without a body. I wouldn't have to go to bed—ever. I would not have to waste time sleeping, cooking and eating, exercising, or doing any other thing that is needed to "take care of" my body. And, the best part would be that my body, the thing that makes me most uncomfortable in the world, and the thing I most hate thinking about, would suddenly be a non-issue. I have fought sleep and ignored my body in almost every possible way, but here I am, as solid as ever. I have let the problem of overweight continue to creep up to the point that once again, I now have a reason to be disgusted and loathe my body. Can I stop this? Or, will the cycle of disgust, loathing, and neglect just continue its fatal spiral?

A friend and I were talking about the subject of body image, and I realized that if I tried to say out loud what I really feel, it would be hard to say, hard for her to hear, and perhaps even harder to believe. I have always hated my body, and I still do. Do others carry around the same kind of loathing?

It doesn't seem to matter much that I know a great deal about how my body got this way. In fact, it is clear that knowing has not changed anything much so far. I still ignore my physical needs and get angry when the body-needs become impossible to ignore. I read somewhere that you cannot treat yourself well, i.e. listen to your physical needs, if you are unkind to yourself. I guess I understand that, but I really don't know how to stop feeling angry and betrayed by the body that perversely ignored the desperate messages I was trying to send it.

I have written elsewhere of my attempts to ignore my father's touch and my failure to control the sexual responses he was determined to elicit. What pleased him in my body petrified and disgusted me.

So, "Fine!" I seem to be saying to my body. "You ignored me. Now I will ignore you!" The fact that I am writing my own death sentence rarely concerns me at all. As a matter of fact, sometimes it feels as though I do what I do and neglect doing the things I should do because it might hasten the end of all my worries. Why would I do anything that would prolong this life? A kind of passive, quiet, subversive suicide.

I often prescribe exercise and healthy nutrition as first courses of action with depressed clients. But I also have to meet a client where she is. Of course, Geri would hear nothing of self-care when she was on a course to self-destruct! Timing is everything. So, I made a mental note to not rush the exercise/nutrition thing. We had other work to do—and lots of it—before she would be ready to actually take care of herself. (Some clients will agree initially to do the self-care behavior, and then healthier ways of thinking follow. But Geri was not one of these clients. Her shame was too deep.)

Geri Henderson & Seanne Emerton

14

Nightmares and Dreams

A year or so ago, a friend and I watched *An Education*, a British film about a teenager attending a girls' school. In so many ways, it reminded me of the British-based girl's school I attended: the focus on final exams, the strict headmistress and teachers who'd been trained in Cambridge and Oxford. School was generally a happy place for me. I was often in trouble, not really major, but now I think that I was quite willing to risk the minor punishments of school in exchange for freedom I could never have at home. Nothing was ever so serious that my parents were called. I made sure of that. My siblings and I were always told, "If you ever get in trouble at school, you will find yourself in even greater trouble at home." I remember vowing with my siblings to never, ever tell on each other.

The film depicted the story of a young girl who is completely taken with the attentions of a cultured, educated, and sophisticated older man. He later turns out to be married, something she discovers just in time to avoid ruining her life. She is counseled by her teachers, admonished by the headmistress, and talked about by her classmates. She drops out of school, and it is another year before she finishes and attends college. The scenarios that played out in this movie were the fears that became my nightmares.

My nightmares include becoming pregnant and suffering public humiliation because I was pregnant (something we were repeatedly warned against in school). Was it because I was often in trouble at school that I had these dreams? Or was it because I was worried that my father used no protection, and neither did I?

Consciously and subconsciously, Geri had to worry about potential pregnancy. There are so many layers of stress that she endured, and endured for a very long time. It is no wonder that she was plagued with nightmares.

Another horrible recurring nightmare was the one I had of my mother dying and my father's decision to marry me. I saw myself, walking up the church aisle in white (*me*, in virginal white?), crying with every step and having no escape. There is no question about where *this* particular nightmare came from! I worried all the time about my mother dying. I was 14 when my mother turned 40. It was one of the most dreadful days of my life. I had imagined that at 40 she was very old and would soon die. Poor Mother! I am quite sure I told her about my fear of losing her soon. She laughed it off as she did so many of our little concerns.

Fear of abandonment and rejection are common themes for incest victims. While her mother was not able to protect Geri from the abuse, she was the primary attachment figure upon whom Geri most depended. The fear of losing her must have been huge.

The other memorable nightmares came during intensive parts of my therapy. One night I awoke, my eyes wide open, and saw my sister lying beside me, dead. I cried and cried. Another night I awoke, sat up, and started fighting a net that I thought was dropping over me from the ceiling. I screamed and fought, without ever really waking up, convinced it was real. Once, I thought I awoke to see my father sitting in the chair across from my bed, and I screamed. When the intensity of therapy diminished, my nightmares diminished and were never as frightening again. As a matter of fact, I don't really remember much about my dreams now. Usually, it feels as though there is a big, black hole at night.

It is not unusual for the intensity in dream life to coincide with intensity happening in therapy. Dreams can be highly informative of the work the subconscious (renowned dream analyst, Dr. Carl Jung, referred to it as the unconscious) is doing in an effort to assist us consciously. This is because a dream frequently compensates the dreamer's conscious attitude as we work through what is known as our "shadow" material (everything about ourselves of which we are not conscious). Nightmares often are shadow material in our unconscious mind. This means they offer an opportunity for us to look deeper into what is consciously trying to get our attention. Dreams can help our attitudes or our feeling state self-regulate. Plus, dreaming serves its various functions whether we are aware of it or not. Geri was obviously working through her deepest fears and her trauma of sexual abuse during her dream time. Dreams are designed to help us by bringing to our consciousness and our ego state those things we try to push down. They are part of the "body/psyche's self-regulatory nature...as dreaming consolidates memories and lessons we have learned to insure survival as well as psychic equilibrium."[4] So, while nightmares are unpleasant to experience, it is the body/mind's way of restoring balance and of helping us work out our issues. The discussion in therapy centers around how the dream trying to help. What is it trying to say? Geri would often do this kind of reflection on her own. Noticing dreams and writing them down offers a deepened way of working consciously with the material that is so rich within all of us.

Dreams are a great self-awareness tool that, when noticed and honored by paying attention to them, can help us work on our issues, lessening the likelihood of them being projected onto others.

---

4   Tyas, Howard. (2011) "Wisdom of the Dream: A Jungian Approach to Dream Interpretation." http://www.trainingandseminars.com/product_print. asp?productID=5622anddeltype=9andstate=MOandcity=St%20Louisandv-enueID=67946

15

Lost

I get lost.
I don't see my surroundings.
I don't know right from left.
I have no sense of North, South, East or West.
So, I get lost.
I lose things.
I don't remember faces.
I get lost.

I don't remember when I realized the seriousness of this, but several incidents have helped me understand that it goes way beyond simply "forgetting" or even just getting "turned around." It's more of a not-knowing. What it means is that I'm never really sure until I'm in my own neighborhood that I am going where I want to go. All the landmarks that might help me know where I am look brand new the next time I see them. Sometimes they all look the same. I don't mind when I'm alone, but when someone is with me, well, it becomes a bigger deal. This becomes obvious by their stupefaction when "going back the way we came" is impossible for me to do without reading the directions backwards, turning the map upside-down, or being given help of some kind. Most of my friends now know that it is not enough to say, "Turn right at the next light." As a matter of fact, it's fairly useless to me. To say, "turn on my side at the next light" is a much more effective direction. Recently, a visiting friend and I drove back and forth on a street looking for a grocery store. Was it before this or that coffee shop, beauty salon, market? After the fifth time and then finding the store closed, my friend announced, "Oh my! This is worse than I thought." Indeed.

In Geri's words, she's "never been more lost than found," so she gets by with this distracting "lostness." "In the end," she says," you do find your way!" She likes quoting one of her favorite lines from the film The Best Exotic Marigold Hotel: "Everything will be okay in the end, and if it's not okay, it's not the end!" Things work out for Geri. I don't think that's an accident. She builds relationships and treats people with great respect. She's not afraid to ask for help, and people want to help her. (I must say she also seems to have a fair amount of luck and/or grace when it comes to finding herself, her way, or whatever she has lost.)

Another problem with having almost no visual memory is that I keep losing things. Seanne and I once worked on "mindfulness": being present in the moment. Is that the problem? Not being attentive to what is currently going on? Always thinking of the next thing? Lots of people do that, I think. But to be so unaware that I cannot remember where anything is if it's not where it belongs means spending big chunks of time looking for things. Some things, like being lost, losing things, and being unaware are annoyances, but they are not life-and-death issues; they do not bring on depression. On the contrary, they can be amusing. The trick is to try not taking them too seriously. Recently, Seanne and I had a discussion about mindfulness. I told her it was boring to have to try to pay attention all the time (also impossible, really). If I have to use all my energy to be attentive, then I don't have any head space left for thinking about fun things or problem-solving!

Geri is the first to admit that she chooses not to work on this issue of mindfulness as she actually finds it rather entertaining to go about rather lost. Her well-honed sense of humor contributes greatly to what I call her Resiliency Factor. She keeps herself well entertained! Yet, as we discussed in Chapter 11 ("Body, Mine?"), Geri's abuse history certainly contributes to her wanting to deny her body. It's understandable that she does not sense a specific space of herself in the world. As long as she denies she belongs in the world, she acts as if she doesn't matter (physically and emotionally), contributing to her truly lost feeling. She has spent a good majority of her life being highly cerebral or dissociated and not "in her body."

But what is worse is that I cannot remember faces very well, except for those of my closest friends and family. I have made terribly embarrassing mistakes, like the time I saw a lady in the church fellowship hall before a service. I greeted her with, "Oh, my! It's been such a long time. It's so nice to see you." Perhaps it was a long time, perhaps it wasn't, but at least she was gracious—the first time. The second time, less than ten minutes later in the narthex, she was clearly upset, frightened even. She backed up and walked away without a word. It was only during the service that I figured out what had happened and the reason she might have been upset. Even then, I could not recall her face.

As well as being embarrassing, this is particularly problematic when I agree to meet someone in a public place, I have found the best strategy is to look down, praying that whoever it is will see and recognize me. I never want people to know that I cannot recognize them. It seems like an insult somehow.

I do, however, remember what I hear, and that has helped me immeasurably with school, remembering what was said in meetings and whose voice said it. If only people would provide audio-videos when being introduced. Then, as soon as they spoke, their name and the face would click together like puzzle pieces, maybe.

What does any of this have to do with this book? I am not sure. I do know that, as a child, it was important for me to remain oblivious to much that surrounded me and that remembering events of my childhood has taken a great deal of time and energy. Even with all my efforts, I know that there are things I've been told about that I cannot remember. That's fine. I have remembered enough to help me help my therapists figure out the most important answers. However, feeling lost in the world diminishes one's sense of safety and increases one's fear of leaving the safety of the known. I do travel, but I have the largest collections of maps and guidebooks of anyone else I know. I always feel a sense of huge accomplishment when I get back to my hotel or apartment safely.

It's almost as if Geri tests this feeling of being safe in the world. Today, she is a frequent flyer world traveler. It's truly amazing that this "disability" does not hold her back. And, as she suggests, there are many reasons why she probably did not develop a visual sense. It served her well, many times, to remain as oblivious as she could to what has happening to her. On the other hand, Geri's auditory sense has always been highly sensitized, so much so that unpleasant and very loud sounds are extremely distracting and even painful to her.

I've thought a great deal about feeling safe in the world. That is not an easy feeling to acquire. I realize that I have spent most of my life feeling lost, unattached, disconnected, and as if I don't belong. Sometimes, I believe it has to do with growing up overseas. Other times, I believe it has to do with never feeling like a real member of my family.

My father often called me "anti-social" when I preferred to be alone rather than accompany the family on a day trip to the beach. Many times, too, it was clear to everyone that if I hadn't angered my father in some way the rest of the family would have been much calmer and happier. My behavior or whatever it was created unhappiness and discomfort for the rest of the family. I didn't know why I constantly seemed to do things that made life harder for everyone else. It was obvious to me I didn't belong there. I was sure I'd been adopted.

Geri has never felt like she belonged. Even now, with her global network of truly wonderful friends and family, she doesn't seem to settle in and "belong" anywhere. She is a nomad in search of self and safety. Geri has always embraced change. Change offers her the opportunity to remake herself, and Geri's frequent moves give her hope that finally, it will all be okay. She resists "settling down" even though her mind sometimes thinks that is what she really wants. There is an adrenaline rush that accompanies change. Geri is wired for adrenaline as part of her body's stress response. Unfortunately and tragically, this dates back to when her abuse first started.

As mentioned in Chapter 3, when the body/mind is experiencing a stress response, the "fight or flight" reaction is constantly turned on, which causes a physiological ripple effect. "…..Your hypothalamus, a tiny region at the base of your brain, sets off an alarm system in your body. Through a combination of nerve and hormonal signals, this system prompts your adrenal glands, located atop your kidneys, to release a surge of hormones, including adrenaline and cortisol. Adrenaline increases your heart rate, elevates your blood pressure and boosts energy supplies. Cortisol, the primary stress hormone, increases sugars (glucose) in the bloodstream…." [5]

The body's stress response is usually self-regulating and decreases when the perceived threat has passed. However, when stressors of one's life are always present (as they were in Geri's childhood and then thereafter), the

---

5   Mayo Foundation for Medical Education and Research, 1998-2012 http:// www.mayoclinic.com/health/stress/SR00001

stress response stays turned on. Obviously, the long-term effects of this puts a person at increased risk for a number of health issues, including heart disease, sleep problems, digestive problems, depression, and obesity, as we discussed in Chapter 3.

Geri has made great strides in learning and implementing methods for effective stress tolerance. Yet, it's a constant battle, and she has some chronic health issues as a result.

What Seanne said about the "constant battle" is absolutely right on so many fronts! I wonder if that feeling occurs to other survivors of childhood trauma. Sometimes, I think, "Good, I made it to these many years (however many they are at the time). I wonder how many more I have to go before I can die because I'm tired of fighting to make my life work." But that's only sometimes. Most of the time, I'm too busy, like everyone else, putting one foot in front of the other to look back or notice how hard it is.

Geri Henderson & Seanne Emerton

16

Sensitive

Being a sensitive person seems like a good explanation for the way I feel things both physically and emotionally. I think it must be something we're born with. If years of therapy were going to cure this, it should have done so by now.

I used to worry about being so sensitive, deciding I was weak and wishing I could tolerate the pain and suffering I saw in the world. I was envious of the neglect some people seemed to be able to have for the wrongs of the world. But, try as hard as I could, I wept easily, felt real misery for the troubles of others, and could not tolerate books, movies, or stories that were too sad, violent, and frightening.

In the early 1990's, psychologist Elaine Aron, who wrote The Highly Sensitive Person, *estimated that 15 to 20 percent of the population could be characterized as highly sensitive (HS). Such characteristics can include having a great imagination; having great intellectual abilities; being very creative; having a curious mind; being a hard worker and a good problem solver; extremely compassionate, intuitive, caring and spiritual; having a strong sense of aesthetic awareness; respecting nature, art and music greatly; having profound and intense sensations; possessing an ability to access important information from the unconscious mind; and having a depth of understanding, feeling, and the ability to see the big picture. The most re-*

cent article (updated March 25, 2014, Huffington Post*) on highly sensitive people supports Dr. Aron's work.*[6]

Life can be very difficult for these individuals if they do not learn to handle their high sensitivity. They are susceptible to poor stress tolerance for a number of reasons, including the tendency to give too much to others, based on their "highly empathic temperament." This is also known as "empathic distress," meaning the individual cannot tolerate the perceived pain or suffering of another because they over-identify. They often put others' needs before their own, and sometimes the highly sensitive person is not even fully aware of what their own needs are.

Dr. Aron's book was very helpful for Geri because it helped her accept that she indeed has these characteristics, and once we could name it, she could better manage it. The highly sensitive person is easily overstimulated and overwhelmed, so part of managing the symptoms includes learning to step back and finding ways to center oneself. Highly sensitive people often need time and space to be by themselves in order to process the amounts of input they absorb. They may have a low tolerance for too much noise, for instance, and their bodies are often more sensitive as well. Learning to keep their own nervous symptoms steady is key and is the difference between empathic distress and healthy compassion. Learning to have boundaries and to be assertive is also key to managing life. Obviously, these were skills Geri did not master until much later.

I'll never forget my mother's well-intentioned reading list. As I mentioned earlier, I read at a young age so Mother began giving me her selections. Most of the time, I was eager to read everything she gave me. However, there were two books I could not get through for a long time. When I was ten, she gave me *Oliver Twist* and *Black Beauty*. Within a few pages of the Dickens' book, I was weeping for poor Oliver and had to put it down. I tried again at 12 and one last time at 14 before managing to make it to the end. As for *Black Beauty*? I did finish it...sometime, but it was a struggle.

I remember that my sister, Lily, loved to watch the Hitchcock TV series and that even though I was in bed, hearing the music of the show was enough to terrify me. I also remember watching a couple episodes of

6   Sensitive. Feb. 26, 2014, updated Mar. 25, 2014. Chan, Amanda. "16 Habits of Highly Sensitive People." *Huffington Post.*

Twilight Zone, which was two episodes more than I should have seen. I now have my friends tell me which movies to see and which books to read. I have no curiosity about the ones they warn me to avoid. When the Mel Gibson movie, *The Passion of The Christ,* came out, Lily my sister, believed that it was everyone's Christian obligation to see it. I was momentarily irritated. So, we dropped the subject and I never went. The powerful reminders of the Passion during Holy Week and on Good Friday have reduced me to tears many times.

While I didn't know about being hypersensitive until more recent years, I've always felt I was unusually emotional. So when my mother decided I should go off to high school in the States, I prayed not to cry. More than just pray, I promised myself I would not cry, no matter how many good-byes I had to say. I was tired of feeling sad and it seemed to me that if I stopped crying, I wouldn't be sad. It was true—well, at least partly true. My smiling good-byes did make it easier on others, and that was some relief. The problem was that for many years afterward, I felt almost nothing most of the time. Either I felt nothing, or I was depressed. I don't remember a time when I was totally free of the cloud of depression. Of course back in those days, childhood depression was not even recognized, nor would it have been treated on our little island.

Geri was right. Her "smiling goodbyes" mostly helped others. This is another great example of how she subjugated her own needs by putting others first. She also lost, bit by bit, her honesty with self. It was a coping mechanism and allowed her, on one level, to get by and to actually leave home. Yet, I am convinced this denial of feelings contributed to her depression. How would it have played out had she been honest with her feelings? She feels it would have made it harder because others would have suffered more. Seeing those she loved concerned about her sadness in leaving may have been enough for her to beg to stay. Surely, the abuse would have continued had she stayed. Yet again, we see the price she paid by "putting on the face." Depression reared its ugly head and has haunted her for years.

I've often wondered, does being highly sensitive dramatically affect the way a person (both as a child and adult) interprets what is happening? I think it does. I know of others who have (apparently) managed to move on from their traumatic pasts much more quickly than I. I have a theory about memories that seems to hold true for me and for others too. It is this: I cannot remember physical pain. No matter how many migraine headaches I have had, there is no way for me to recall what they feel like. On the other hand, I can easily recall emotional pain. Sometimes, the intensity of my emotional pain even increases with recollection. Left by itself, it seems to grow and eat away at life and joy.

It has taken me a long time to realize that being very sensitive to just about everything—loud noises, sudden movements, big, noisy crowds, physical pain, and everything else that enters my conscious world—has any positive aspects at all. What has become clear to me, however, is that because of my sensitivity, I am usually empathetic with people. I am sensitive to the needs of others and much more understanding of my students and colleagues. People find it easy to talk to me, and coupled with some sense about underlying issues, I can often be helpful. The moment I recognized that, I realized that I would not trade the sometimes painful effects of being sensitive for the beneficial ones that bring closeness and comfort to those around me.

In fact, I would have to say that these days, I am much more appreciative of my sensitivity than annoyed by it. I recognize that the deep and rewarding relationships and friendships I have are directly related to this and the empathy that comes with it. I have learned of ways to protect myself and learned of the limits of my tolerance that must be honored. I have also learned where those limits are so that when I choose to cross them, I do so knowing what the consequences will be.

This made "doing therapy" quite challenging. Her sensitivities often would catch me off-guard as I would plow in and try to take on the treatment plan with her. Then, I would have to laugh at myself because I consider myself highly sensitive as well. Geri was quite skilled at verbally and/ or nonverbally making it clear when she was emotionally satiated with what felt to me to be a painstakingly slow approach. I often had to override my own sensitive qualities to push when I felt it absolutely necessary. For instance, I often wanted to protect Geri from being overwhelmed with her own negative emotions and yet knew it was my job to help move her forward by facing them. It was a balancing act, to say the least.

I find Seanne's comments here to be evocative of the times we spent together—sometimes rewarding, sometimes frustrating. She never told me we were working slowly, but I often sensed that we were. On the other hand, I never felt that Seanne was disappointed with our slow pace even when I was. So, when she says she had to decide to push me at times, I was rarely aware of it as "pushing" but rather as moving forward. It must have been a tricky balance for Seanne to maintain. Had I felt any kind of aggressive "push" on her part, it would have been frightening and yet when she challenged me, I liked the sense that we were making progress.

It is challenging to meet clients where they are and yet also keep forward movement in the therapeutic process. It often feels like a dance in terms of one step forward and then one step back until we are in sync, moving forward together. Sometimes, we are never in the same rhythm, but the dance continues anyway, and sometimes we step on each other's toes. When Geri and I established a relationship with enough trust for direct feedback, we danced in rhythm.

It is not always easy to stay in sync because I am by nature an impatient person and because I don't want clients to suffer longer than needed. I like to choose methods of working with clients that move them forward rather quickly. Of course, timing is everything, and I have to be sensitive to the readiness of the client before proceeding too quickly.

I am trained and certified in using the method of EMDR (Eye Movement Desensitization Reprocessing), which I find moves clients effectively and efficiently through processing trauma. However, it was not appropriate to use at the time, given Geri's history of dissociation and the fact she was still dissociating. I used other cognitive behavioral methods to help Geri integrate positive beliefs to increase her sense of safety and to emotionally self-regulate. As this sense of safety increased (at what seemed to be incremental levels, but still it increased), we were able to process more levels of the trauma, always with the intention of helping Geri feel more compassion than disdain for self. Geri's high sensitivity greatly amplifies her experience of her feelings, be they positive or negative. This was very difficult to combat. Today I would choose to use Dialectical Behavioral Therapy (DBT) [7] and Mindfulness Based Stress Reduction (MBSR)[8] techniques with Geri, as they are evidence based and highly effective methods to manage emotional regulation. I was not yet trained in these modalities at the time.)

---

7   Dialectical Behavior Therapy, a type of cognitive behavioral therapy that teaches behavioral skills to help you tolerate distress, manage or regulate your emotions, and improve your relationships with others. http://www.mayoclinic.org/diseases-conditions/self-injury/basics/treatment/con-20025897

8   Mindfulness Based Stress Reduction, helps you live in the present, appropriately perceive the thoughts and actions of those around you to reduce your anxiety and depression, and improve your general well-being. http://www.mayoclinic.org/diseases-conditions/self-injury/basics/treatment/con-20025897

Geri's perseverance is a powerful strength she possesses. This reduces her sense of helplessness and thereby contributes to her ability to be resilient.[9] She did her homework assignments even when she didn't want to. Her emotional regulation toolbox, such as it was, therefore began to fill with more tools she could use. This helped turn down the volume on some of her high sensitivities so that she could function in the world. (There was a time Geri would only go to the grocery store in the middle of the night so that she wouldn't have to deal with too many people.) By the time treatment with me had ended, not only was Geri able to get groceries at the busiest times of the day, but she also was able to move abroad and start a new job in a new country.

---

9   Martin Seligman, PhD, University of Pennsylvania, did groundbreaking research showing the relationship of feelings of helplessness in traumatized subjects and the break down in the immune system, sometimes resulting in the development of cancer. David Servan-Schreiber, MD, PhD, in *Anti-cancer, A New Way of Life* (Viking, 2009) discusses this physiology of helplessness and how critical it is to develop an attitude and behaviors of management to combat the helplessness. Therefore practicing perseverance, optimism and effective mood regulation reinforces the resilient spirit, allowing a mentality of survivorship rather than victimization.

17

The Purpose Driven Life

Our church read and studied a book together, *The Purpose Driven Life.*[10] Chapter 2 is titled, "You Are Not an Accident." That's appealing, but the chapter ends with this poem:

> You are who you are for a reason,
> You're part of an intricate plan.
> You're a precious and perfect unique design,
> Called God's special woman or man.

> (So far, so good. Maybe I believe this, not sure any more.)

> You look like you look for a reason,
> Our God made no mistake,
> He knit you together within the womb,
> You're *just* what he wanted to make.

> (Hmm...I don't think all the genetic malformations found in embryos can be blamed on God.)

> The parents you had were the ones he chose,
> And no matter how you may feel,
> They were custom-designed with God's plan in mind,
> And they bear the Master's seal.

---

10   Rick Warren, Zondervan, 2002.

(Uh-oh! I don't think even my parents would have been happy about this one. The more I read this verse, the more flawed it seems to me! Does God custom-design abusive parents? Really? Isn't that like blaming sin on God?)

No, that trauma you faced was not easy,
And God wept that it hurt you so;
But it was allowed to shape your heart
So that into his likeness you'd grow.[11]

Russell Kelfer
(No! What kind of God is this?)

So, back into therapy *and* the minister's office I went to figure this out. The idea of it seems to be that God allows trauma for ultimate good. I don't believe that. I finally decided this poem is not meant for everyone; it certainly was not meant for me. I do not see how abuse shapes our hearts into the likeness of God. Abuse that supposedly shapes people for good or, more precisely, into the likeness of God, just makes me angry. I do, however, believe that God does not interfere where people's free will is concerned. That's why people keep hurting each other. But if I am spiritually aware, I believe that God can help me become someone who can use her experiences to help others, someone who might have a special sensitivity for the hurts of others.

I clearly remember the therapy session after Geri read this. She was devastated. It's as if reading this poem confirmed all she had believed about herself: that she somehow deserved and was even preordained to be abused by her father. It was highly challenging to combat this with Geri. Her church sanctioned this book, after all. It felt like we were back at square one with all the shame issues. All the cognitive/behavioral work in the world was challenged with this unfortunate experience. She wept most of the session, and I sat with her. I encouraged her to speak to her minister since I knew I had no credibility in this department, not being her minister and not of her denomination. I also knew her minister and knew him to be a reasonable, intelligent, and caring individual.

Thank God, her minister said he understood what she was saying and was highly empathic toward her. He thanked Geri for letting him know because he was sure he would hear from others on it. He let her know that

---

11   Warren, pp. 25-6.

he understood that the poem itself wasn't appropriate and was not "God's Word." My session alone with Geri would not have done it without this intervention from Geri's spiritual advisor. Because of his conversation with Geri, however, she was able to move forward. It's a great example again of how the right words from the right person make all the difference in the world.

18

Security, Safety!

I have traveled quite a bit in the last several years and have had to pass through airport security many times. This has caused me huge anxiety. I have had to apologize to security agents whom I have mistreated in my anger and my displeasure about their search process. During one particularly difficult time when I was battling severe depression, I went to see a friend. Using my free miles, I was routed all over the United States to end up in British Columbia. No matter what measures I took, I was searched at each airport. By the time I got to the West Coast, I was completely undone. I called Seanne's office and begged to be put through to her. I didn't think I could get through one more security check to my destination.

Looking back, I am not sure what I thought she could do from such a distance, but in that moment Seanne's calming voice and advice was what I needed to hear. She told me that for now, I should ignore the whole process (dissociate). Then, she added that if I ever told anyone she said that, she'd deny it! Well, it worked and was probably the only thing that would have worked as a long-distance technique.

This was a desperate time for Geri. She had to get through security, and she was all alone. While I was concerned about coaching her to consciously dissociate which, by the way, also included instruction on how to ground herself especially on the phone and not in the safety of my office, I knew at this stage of therapy that this was likely the only way to get her through. The key was making it a conscious choice, something she could control and invite willingly. Her previous pattern had been to "just let it happen." Later, Geri reported surprise that she could manage the dissociation rather than the dissociation managing her. It turned out to be an empowering intervention for her and one she still chooses to use when a desperate need presents itself.

Why is going through airport security causing me so much anxiety? This has been hard for me to figure out, but realizing that I had to write about it, I started paying attention to the details involved with being searched. I realized that it is hard because I must submit to being touched as if I'm being "felt up" without choice and without complaint. I have to be compliant in the hands of someone else. In this situation, too, the stakes are too high to resist the intrusions. I have found that watching security officers dig through my carry-ons is trying. It feels like another kind of violation.

In these situations, Geri is once again experiencing a lack of control over her own body, and she is caught in a "no way out" position. Of course it causes her anxiety. She is just now paying enough attention to her body that she can sort out the details. Her pattern has been to deny how the body feels, "just do it" and get it over with. This has not allowed her the opportunity for mindfulness: just to notice her body and the accompanying cognitions, like what she is telling herself. Now, when she recognizes an irrational thought, like "I am not safe," she can catch it and change it to a rational thought, such as "I am safe."

Figuring this out has not taken all my airport anxiety away, especially overseas, but I am not quite as disgusted by being wanded and touched. I still must mentally prepare for each walk through security and at times have to take my mind away from what is really going on. Perhaps, this isn't really dealing with the situation in the best sense of the word, but it gets me through. I also come ready with footies for my feet and no metal of any kind anywhere on me.

Seanne recently told me about a new TSA service. The last time I traveled, I called the number. After overhearing my side of the conversation, Seanne realized that I wasn't getting the kind of response I should have. She wrote: Say, "I am a PTSD incest survivor." I gulped and then, in a rush of words, made myself say it out loud to a stranger. I thought I would collapse, but, when I didn't, I realized that the person at TSA Cares had immediately changed his attitude. He told me that he would do his best to alert staff at the regional and Chicago airports but that I needed to give them about 72 hours' notice in the future. I thanked him and hung up, so grateful the call was over and so relieved that I might not face the same treatment in the future, at least in the USA. Within a few minutes, a local TSA representative called me, told me the name of the person I should look for in the regional airport, and left me her personal cell number in case I needed anything else. I thanked her. Both Seanne and I were amazed at the responsive and caring support of the TSA. I wondered what would happen in Chicago, where my biggest fears have always been realized. The Chicago TSA has always been gruff, grumpy, power-hungry, and proud of it, in my experience!

The next day I arrived at the first airport in plenty of time and met a friend for coffee after checking in. Closer to boarding time, I approached the TSA Security people and asked for the name I'd been given. Everyone pointed to her, and she waved. I went back to my friend to visit a little longer, but when I approached the checkpoint again, the designated officer came over immediately, invited my friend to stay with me, and made sure I had placed everything in the bins correctly before going through the scanner. When there were no alarm bells, it seemed to me that every TSA officer let out a sigh of relief. (I'm sure I heard that!) I could tell that my anxiety would be completely absent for future flights as long as this procedure is in place. I *will* call 3 days ahead. I absolutely will!

I have made a promise to myself that I will not, ever again, fly in the US without alerting the Passenger Support Specialist Officer of the TSA! What a huge difference that made. What was interesting to me after the fact was that I found I was much calmer and in better spirits for the long flight overseas than I had been in years. I have always been aware of the fact that the travelling experience, from security to flight, is one of having to sit in closer proximity to your seatmate than you would even with your family. Negative TSA experiences have always made me want to try to disappear, crawl into my seat, and become a non-person, but that's impossible to do, of course.

I had an emotional response overhearing Geri's conversation with the TSA agent once she had told him her diagnosis and he started taking her seriously. (We were no longer in the therapist/client relationship and were in the process of writing this book at the time this call was made.) I had almost given up hope that anything would really change for her. I had walked with her so closely regarding this part of her journey that I was overwhelmed with relief, hope, and gratitude when her experience went well. It was powerful for her to actually not only be heard, but to be taken seriously, and then treated with respect. She travels so much, and to think how she had suffered prior to this new experience made me even more aware of the depth and breadth of the negative ripple effect her abuse history had created. To think that the TSA Passenger Support Specialist Officer has the power to make such a positive difference in someone's life is not only hopeful but redemptive.

I am incredibly grateful for our own community's TSA agent who brought this awareness to me so I could share it with Geri. This officer is passionate about her work and determined to do her part in creating a caring, competent TSA team even beyond her own city. She has since notified the TSA agents in both Omaha and Chicago how well the Passenger Support Specialist services worked for Geri. I hope this will be a widely publicized service so others can benefit as Geri has. The positive effects of proactive intervention such as the Passenger Support Specialist provided, expand exponentially. For instance, in this situation, Geri had much less anxiety, was less frazzled, and was more present in her body as she prepared to board the plane. Geri is a seasoned traveler and does not create issues for flight attendants, but other passengers with a trauma history very well could and undoubtedly do. It will not only serve passengers with PTSD well, but it will also well serve the airlines and airports to keep this Passenger Support Specialist program strong and well utilized.

My update for another venture into the world of TSA Cares is the experience I had in Chicago recently. I called ahead and gave them all my information and times of arrival at O'Hare and departure. However, when I arrived in the international terminal to transfer to the other terminals for US flights, I could find no one in security who understood "Passenger Support Specialist" when I asked. I was sent from one end of the terminal to the other and even to a ticketing agent. Of course, I knew that wasn't right. Finally, a supervisor was called over, and he found the person who was supposed to help. She was very kind, very patient, and very helpful, but putting someone in the body scanner is not my idea of sensitivity to the needs of traumatized passengers. I was in tears by the time I had emerged and claimed my things.

Much later, in the United lounge, I received a call from an agent looking for me. Apparently they had not received my arrival information or, according to him, they would have met my flight, taken me through passport control, customs, and security on the other end. That would have been perfect. Until recently, I have had to repeat, "I am a PTSD Incest survivor" every time I call. Apparently, they now have a database with personal information connected to my phone number and email address. I can still get in trouble when I don't pay close attention to the individual systems of each airport. They are not the same, and missing a step can still result in another traumatic experience. Agents, though, seem to be willing to do whatever they can to help improve systems.[12]

---

12   TSA Cares 855-787-2227

19

I Want To Die

I wasn't very old when I began to dream about dying. As I mentioned earlier, my first remembered nightmare was that my mother would die and leave me to marry my father and look after my siblings.

How I wish there would have been earlier therapeutic intervention with Geri! Obviously, these dreams would be a big red flag to a therapist. These are not dreams of a child living a happy, healthy childhood.

But the most comforting dreams were ones in which I did die. Awake or asleep, I was convinced everyone would be happy for me to be gone. Most of the time, I felt like the whole family agreed with Father: I was bad; I deserved to be beaten; I was always causing trouble. So, surely everyone would rejoice when the house became peaceful and quiet because I wasn't there. I knew something else that no one but my father knew—I would die a horrible sinner because of what he had done and because I hadn't been able to stop him or even stop my own body from participating.

I prayed hard for forgiveness, believing also that at any moment Christ's Second Coming would take my family away, leaving me alone. I experienced sheer panic the few times I arrived home and found no one home. It had happened. Jesus had come, and I had been *Left Behind.* (I've never read that series, by the way, knowing it would probably bring back those horrible fears.)

Geri's perception of herself was anchored in her experiences with her father. He treated her like an object, a worthless, unlovable object. So, of course, Geri believed that she was "bad" and "deserved to be beaten." The longer she kept the sexual abuse secret, the more Geri's personal narrative of being a "horrible sinner" grew. It was made all the more complicated by her body's natural responses, causing her shame to compound and solidifying her belief that there was no one to blame but herself. It became impossible for her to see that it was her father who was at fault and that she was a good soul. What could be worse for a child? It was bad enough that there was no escape for Geri from the reality that she had to live, but when she layered the sinner concept over it, her life became truly hopeless in her eyes.

Barring the fate of the horrible sinner, I hoped to die. I never had an actual suicide plan until much later, but early on, my hope to die was a wish and a prayer. I believed for many years, well into adulthood, that my prayer wasn't answered because God didn't even want me in heaven or didn't love me enough to answer my prayer. Even now, I sometimes think about my age and try to figure out how much longer I have to try to stay here and make my life work. Will it be 10, 15, 20, 25, or 30 more years? I hope not! I no longer fear that I am going to Hell. Rather, I want what "eternal rest" would mean for me. It sounds wonderful!

Geri's death wish became her only escape route. I was appalled early in our therapy work when Geri announced her life plan was to die before the age of 60. At least, by the time she reached me, she most often wished for natural causes of death and was not actively suicidal. However, her desire to die an early death did work against any hope of a successful self-care plan! (As I mentioned, I often prescribe exercise and healthy nutrition as first courses of action with depressed clients. But Geri had another agenda!)

I was in my late 20s, living in Nebraska, when I began to think seriously about dying. I started to think about how to manage it and what methods would be successful. I treated the whole exercise of developing a suicide plan as if it were an interesting puzzle to solve. I addressed each problem I ran into and ended up with a very complicated scenario. First, I would drive somewhere to a remote location where no one would find me for a long time. (I had many daily interactions with both adults and children in my work, and I didn't want anyone I knew to be traumatized by finding me.) Then, I would take handfuls of drugs washed down with alcohol, cover up with a blanket and just go to sleep in the backseat of the car. By the time anyone discovered my decomposed body, they wouldn't be able to tell what had really happened to me. Then, no one would feel guilty about what they should have known or done.

This is a well-developed suicide plan, which in and of itself, is a measurement of high risk. I don't find it coincidental that Geri's depression deepened when she moved to the Midwest. She had grown up on a beautiful tropical island and also had lived in major cities. Our state was a cultural vacuum compared with what Geri had been accustomed to and therefore was highly isolating for her. However, when she lost her job and her apartment in another state, Geri called her parents out of desperation. They found her a job opportunity, and she found herself here, living again in close proximity to her original abuser. She was no longer able to hide. Inescapable contact with her father, isolation, and the absence of cultural activities all combined created the perfect storm, for Geri.

In the meantime, I got into the habit of drinking every night. I would close the curtains, sit in the dark, and not answer the phone or the door. I also slept and ate very irregularly while I planned my death and, all the while, continued to work. I discovered later that parents of students who saw me during this time thought I'd lost a family member. But I laughed off every question about what was wrong. Finally, a concerned friend told a psychologist we both knew that she thought I was in trouble. He came and banged on the door one night, threatening to bring the police and even break the door down! I let him in and, in a few minutes, found myself throwing a few things into a bag to be taken to the hospital. I was there for three weeks.

Of course, Geri kept her suicide plan a secret so no one really knew. What she failed to recognize, given her state of mind, was that her friends were quick to notice her declined state. Thank God!

So, while she was in the perfect storm for deepening depression, she also was in a space (literally) to finally look at and deal with what she had been running from all these years. She seemed a stubborn soul to me at times, but this perception may have been my own inability to fully understand the multiple layers of issues that blocked her in moving forward. Unfortunately, it took her more than one hospitalization and more than one therapist to finally be ready to deal with the demons.

(Seanne says I seemed "a stubborn soul." But by the time I got to her office, I was wary and tired. I knew she was trying her best to help me, and I believed I was trying my best to cooperate and do what she asked. But my internal "war" made it difficult. It's hard, even for me, to understand how my desire to get better could be so thwarted by fear.)

There were a few funny incidents during this first hospital stay. For a start, I hadn't bothered to specify any one religious denomination, so I became fair game for every minister who made rounds. It was the hospital Chaplain, Sr. Sophia Rose though, who really puzzled me. She came in looking very grim. Then, she looked at me and shook her head. "Geri, it doesn't look good."

"It doesn't?" I asked hopefully.

"No, it doesn't."

After some minutes of watching her doleful face, I said, "Sister, are you going to pray for me or what?"

"Oh! Well, okay," she said and bowed her head. She read one of her prayer cards and handed it to me when she finished. Then she left and never returned.

Another day, I decided I'd had enough of morning and evening therapy sessions and would leave. I knew that wherever I went, a nurse would ask, "Where are you going?" So, I just put my coat on and walked out the side door closest to my room. While this hospital had no psych ward, it had been made clear to everyone why I was there and that I was not to leave. Since I have a terrible sense of direction, I headed directly away from the hospital as quickly as I could, walking straight into the parking lot of the clinic close by where my doctors all practiced. Caught!

One of them drove up, "Geri, can I give you a lift?"

"Uhmmm... Okay," I mumbled, knowing that she knew where I belonged. By the time I'd returned, my therapist was there waiting for me, not pleased.

Being in the hospital conflicted with a presentation I was scheduled to give to a women's group in my town about the island where I'd grown up, its dialect, culture, and literature. Since the friend who'd scheduled me to present didn't want to tell anyone the real reason I was in the hospital, my therapist (who knew and trusted my friend) let her pick me up, take me, and bring me back. My friend said later that her biggest fear was that I'd do or say something off-the-wall that she'd have to try to explain. I didn't. It went well. That same friend also came one evening and took me to a concert, which was wonderful. I see now that I needed these small outings outside of the hospital to help me try to re-enter my work world.

I spent an additional two weeks living in the home of one of my doctors with his family because I was not allowed to be alone. After a total of five weeks, I was able to return home. It was so very strange and difficult to try to manage things and figure out a new normal, one that included regular meals, sleeping, and a structured schedule. Of course, I was on medication and felt foggy-brained most of the time. I wanted to work, but instead of feeling better, I felt very fragile, unable to go shopping for more than five minutes at a time. When I did return to work, I tried to do so without saying much about where I'd been. I found out later that the local gossip was that I'd been "drying out" after an alcoholic binge! Generally, though, people were pleased I had returned to work and didn't seem to question me much.

After my release from the hospital, my therapist and I continued with outpatient sessions at least once a week and sometimes more often. They were helping somewhat, but I always felt more ill after a therapy session than before. Eventually, I extricated myself from his care, but it was not easy. He kept threatening to tell the authorities that I was not safe alone, that he could prove that I was unbalanced, and that I would be locked up if I didn't keep coming to every session.

I was hospitalized two more times under the care of my second therapist before I figured out that I could not hide my depressed state and my suicidal plans from any therapist worth his/her salt. By the time I had a solid plan and a space of time to do it, I was already being carted off to the hospital. I would have to learn to look and act much more cheerful, whatever my plans! I ran into another snag, too. Often, the medications I was on were so strong I didn't feel much like doing anything, never mind carrying out a complicated suicide plan.

Nowadays, the thought of suicide is usually just a rare escape for me. When life seems miserable and hard and depression sets in, I think, "What if I could just die? Wouldn't that be nice?" I rarely go so far as to have a plan although sometimes I come very close. It is, however, a "when all else fails" safety net that Seanne seems to understand I need. She has never said, "You can't," but, of course, there were always contingency promises to keep—and I did.

This constant death wish was/is part of Geri's reality. It was very difficult for me to accept that this is a part of her that will probably always be. For years, I pondered the best way to deal with it. She was so good at "put-

ting on the face" that she could easily act as if she was okay and safe just to avoid hospitalization. Obviously, it was impossible to work effectively with her therapeutically if she was not going to be honest. I decided I needed to help her feel safe in being able to process her suicidal thoughts verbally with the hope that this would help her deal with her choices rationally. She needed to know I would not hospitalize her the minute she talked about her suicidal thoughts. (Yet, she also knew that if she were indeed serious about executing her plan, I would have to hospitalize her.) While the suicidal ideation was a constant, her level of intent vacillated. This especially became true as she took on an active parenting role with her niece. She was able to have empathy for the impact her death would have on her niece even if she had underestimated the many others whose lives would be traumatized by her death. Geri certainly has had the potential for harm to herself at times where I did not make the choice to have her hospitalized. We always discussed (and she agreed to) safety plans, but I knew she was only humoring me. I had to constantly discern her seriousness about carrying out her death wish. She could not live her life in the hospital. And, unfortunately, the choices of hospitals for her were limited. I frequently sought clinical supervision on Geri's case, but in the end, I had to do what I felt best at the time.

We worked very hard in therapy to increase Geri's repertoire of cognitive/behavioral skills. I pushed her hard at times. There were sessions where she was quite angry with me, and I was certain she would fire me.

I was concerned I would lose her either to suicide or by her just quitting. Yet, I had to do my job. Many times, she wanted me to just agree with her and not push her. The most challenging times were when she was in her child ego state and she went into the "victim role." It felt very manipulative—it was manipulative—but not out of malicious intent. She truly didn't know better. Once she built her skill set to grow her wise mind/adult self-ego state, we made much faster therapeutic progress.

Working with Geri forced me to learn to manage and live with the anxiety of uncertainty. I often felt like I didn't know what I was doing. It was very difficult to have a well-defined treatment plan. I had a big-picture treatment plan, but the interventions varied to meet the need at the time. The therapy tool box had to be quite large so the appropriate intervention could be pulled out in the moment at the right time. She demanded (and deserved, as all clients do) authenticity, responsiveness, and total presence. I often wished I could press a "pause" button in the middle of a session and rush out of the room to consult a colleague on what to do next on how to handle the sudden turns the road had taken. But, of course, that wasn't possible—unlike my family therapy training days when I had the luxury of a trainer and colleagues behind the one way mirror. Further, I had to act like I knew what I was doing because if Geri sensed at all how unsure of myself I actually felt, she would not have felt safe.

I was actually certain Seanne would fire *me*! I never could have guessed she was uncertain. As a matter of fact, the change I needed in a therapist was to have one who let me know she had a plan. What had been frustrating to me in previous therapeutic modes was that I seemed to be the one setting the agenda, but that was impossible because I knew very well that I was the one who was lost. Seanne offered not only a plan but also clear direction and guidance.

I had successfully worked with many victims of sexual/physical and emotional abuse prior to Geri's case. I knew I had the skills. Yet, trusting myself is not always easy. Geri was at high risk. She was/is an intelligent, sensitive, gifted woman and had a stubborn habit of putting others first. Her disgust for self was extreme and her shame level highly toxic. She seemed quite fragile, perhaps due to the extensive abuse history, the lack of consistently good therapy, and her highly sensitive nature. She also had very well-developed defense mechanisms which were like a paper fortress—very visible but ineffective. However, if I blew the paper down and left her exposed before she was ready, she would have collapsed. So, offering clear direction and guidance had to be tempered with what I call "holding space" with Geri. It was a dance between sitting with her and not only acknowledging her pain but also being compassionate with it, as well as offering hope and the sense that there was a way for her to move forward even when she felt so lost.

20

Anger

I've always wondered why I've never felt the kind of anger I've always heard about—the kind of anger I'm supposed to feel toward my father and even toward my mother. I've had to deal with anger, but it is rarely directed toward my family. Instead, the anger I felt was

anger at Little Geri for being the kind of girl who attracted all this trouble and has caused me endless amounts of trouble all my life;

anger at having to retell my story over and over to one therapist after another and anger that it *is* My Story; and

anger at myself for lacking the kind of self-control or willpower to stay healthy and at the appropriate weight.

But full-blown anger at my parents? I do not remember feeling that even when I was being encouraged to try to get in touch with something that would feel like anger. I don't think it was a silly idea I might have had about forgiveness, either.

Instead, I have found myself irrationally angry with retailers, customer service people, and others, so totally lacking in grace and kindness that it is embarrassing and I have had to return to apologize! Once I recognized this as a pattern, I tried hard to make sure to be ready to hear, "Sorry, we cannot help" especially in my overseas life where a customer service culture is unknown in most places.

Of course, Geri denies anger. She was not allowed to express it, and she will say she was not allowed to feel it. I am convinced she did feel it. She must have had rage. Yet, she is a fast learner and a dutiful daughter so she very quickly learned to ignore it and push it down. It was not safe for her to feel or show anger. She would have been physically abused had she done so. She got so good at denying it, not putting it squarely on her father's shoulders, that she developed an automatic response of not feeling it, instead turning the anger inward (which leads to depression), feeling afraid and that something was wrong with her. Geri most often expressed fear, which is the primary tool of the perpetrator. But the anger didn't go away—it came out sideways, to innocent souls and to herself. Her shame compounded. Shame keeps a victim silent. Her lack of assertiveness fed her inability to express any emotion or need directly. All of this has contributed to making her life even harder.

It's true that we were not allowed to express anger or frustration. Losing one's temper was simply not an option. The punishment at our house could be severe for any display of anger. My brother, sister, and I recall that our arguing, especially within earshot of my parents, was always subdued, whispered exchanges that went something like

"Stop it."
"I didn't do anything."
"Yes, you did!"

It would have been difficult to tell how angry we were. At night, we invariably apologized to one another, taking the Scripture verse, "Do not let the sun go down upon your anger" (Eph. 4:26), to heart.

It is interesting, but not really surprising, that this chapter on anger is one of the last ones Geri thought of writing. (And even then, she was reluctant to address it!)

Depression is anger turned inward so obviously we know where Geri's anger went. She's still on medication. Does that mean her work is not complete?

Of course, that's what it means. I know and admit that. What I realize now, after we launched into this topic, is that my fear of anger is pervasive. I am afraid of my own anger and even when a friend or family member does something that might cause me to be angry, I quickly figure out ways to justify their behavior and make it my own fault. And, I am afraid of the anger of others. I will do almost anything to avoid it, trying hard to make sure people are okay with what I say or do.

Geri sometimes has what she calls feelings that are "too unmanageable" so she just walks away. Yet, there are no more episodes of her irrationally lashing out verbally to the undeserving. She began to seriously work on behaviorally managing her sideways expressions of anger with her first overseas therapist. She has made great progress as her assertiveness has significantly improved. Additionally, her health is better, and she is losing weight because she is taking better care of herself in general. Her migraines are much less frequent. This could be a sign that she is not denying her anger and working effectively on core issues of fear and shame. Yet, she persists in not wanting to attend to the emotion of anger. At times, she still gets migraines. This "work on self" is a lifelong project for all of us. I am grateful that as we write this book, Geri currently is in therapy with a highly competent and well trained therapist. That continues to allow us to keep clean lines as colleagues and friends as we talk about the tough issues still present, including displaced anger.

21

Shame

What an ugly, heavy word! This topic and the discussion of it have always made me feel shame all over again—even when I know, rationally, it should not be there! There's something so resonant in that word that it seems to want to drag me back into it. I have to remind myself that I left most of that behind me quite some time ago. I have been trying to remember what it was like when shame was so closely connected with fear that I could hardly tell the difference. The struggle of my family over my disclosure has forced me to try to think about this again and has brought it to the forefront as the main subject of this section. It is an emotion so familiar that I walk back into its prison walls with ease without noticing the doors slamming behind me—again.

What was always so frightening was that my shame over what had happened to me created a lingering sense of guilt that turned into a sense of foreboding that someday, someone would find out what I had done (as yet unnamed crimes) and I would end up on the front page of the newspaper or the lead story of the evening news. It wasn't that I could put my finger on what I had done or might do. I was certain that I would do something awful and bring everlasting shame and embarrassment on myself and my family. I realize that those feelings of fear are mostly gone and that I no longer expect to be publicly humiliated for something I've done.

I was encouraged and even required as homework by my first therapist to start telling my story to my friends. I was told that telling it, saying it out loud, would prove to me that it was not my fault. Further, the more I was able to verbalize it, the weaker the power of the story and the lies would be. The "light outside the prison" would diminish the power of shame over me, scattering the dark shadows that prisons hold within them, creating light in the dark corners where the unspeakable had lived.

But telling was terrible. I held my breath. I would avoid the "I" word, "incest." I would get very cold and shiver. I could not look in the eyes of my friends or even in their direction. And, I waited to see which of my friends would leave me. I imagined they'd say, "You're a disgusting girl. Please, don't come around anymore. We don't want our children associating with you, either." I wouldn't have been surprised.

But not one of my friends deserted me in those first days of dreadful shame. Not one. They didn't treat me differently. They didn't stop coming for lessons. They didn't stop inviting me to their houses. It was quite a revelation, but so much more than that, as I look back on it. It was amazingly healing. I had lived within those walls for such a long time that it is only now, as I have been trying to think about the difference between then and now, that I understand and realize what freedom I have. Each new day no longer brings with it the dread of what might happen that will reduce me to shame and humiliate my family. It's been a long time since I felt that way.

Would it have been different for me if I had read a book about this? Would it have helped to know that disclosure reduces shame and fear? I would like to think so. Coming out of the darkness of fear and secrecy is such an important step in healing, but I remember how very angry I was about having to talk. Being abused was enough, wasn't it? It felt as though being required to talk about it was another form of abuse. It felt like the story was hurting me in multiple layers, again and again, every time I had to share it. I would yell, "This is not my fault, and I don't want to talk about it!"

I realize that accepting God's grace was another, later step. It was much harder to believe that God loved me and didn't blame me for what had happened. At first, I was too ashamed to pray, too ashamed to believe that He could still love me. After all, my father was a minister, and if he said I was a very bad girl, what would God say?

It has taken me a long time to accept the gift of unconditional love from anyone and, most of all, from God. I used to say that my only motivating emotion was fear, I never realized how that restricted my ability to live a normal life until I began to emerge from it. A long time in a small prison is crippling. And just like physical disability, learning to live in an open, new world of confidence and acceptance was not going to be a matter of simply throwing open the prison doors. Rehabilitation meant working hard to believe what I read and heard. Physically and emotionally, my mind had to change.

Yes, shame underlies it all. Shame becomes part of the core of an incest victim. When I ask where it resides most in the body, many victims say their gut, and Geri has always said her tummy. Sometimes, the shame feels very large, and, when asked to describe it, victims often describe it as a big shape, sometimes smaller, depending upon triggering events. (There is abundant research on the "gut/mind" connection and how our thoughts trigger physiological responses in the body, including, of course, the stress response we discussed earlier.) Most survivors say the shame never really goes away. We can hope for skilled management of it, of course, and today Geri most often succeeds in this. However, the choice to publish this book using her real name brought many of the shame issues to the forefront again. It had been so long since she had felt the sting of shame and fear to this extent that it caught her off guard.

She is now more aware that shame is always present to a certain extent, just below the surface. I used to like to believe it was possible to completely shrink it. Now, I'm more inclined to see it as an undercurrent that needs recognized and embraced, even, to notice it without judgment, accept it as part of oneself, and then let it go in the moment so it does not overwhelm one. But letting go of it in the moment is tricky. It requires constant vigilance. It's like standing guard at a gate and noticing its presence but not letting it in. It requires compassion for oneself and then gentle soothing to restore equanimity when shame is knocking. Sometimes, I ask clients to visualize what shame looks, sounds, and feels like to them, its shape, size, color, texture, sound, and temperature. Then, I invite them to visualize a light stream coming from that which is greater than themselves, entering the top of their head with healing light, indeed shrinking the shame in the moment and filling them with healing energy.[13] Some people respond to this as an effective self-soothing technique; others do not.

Managing shame is so key in the healing process and such a constant presence that it requires clients to have a big tool box handy with a variety of tools available that resonate in the moment. It is best practice to also

---

13   Shapiro, Francine. (1995). *Eye Movement Desensitization and Reprocessing.* The Guildford Press: NY. (p. 239).

have a "shame management system" in place proactively even if shame is not knocking loudly at the moment. This system includes whatever works for the client in terms of helping one feel compassion for self so the choice to self-soothe appropriately comes naturally.

One of the best evidence-based practices is yoga. It literally brings awareness of body/mind in the moment and soothes the central nervous system.[14] Consciously doing any kind of body movement activity is great for healing and staying healthy, both emotionally, and physically. The key is doing it with awareness, whether it be golfing, yoga, running, receiving massage or Reiki treatments, dancing, or walking mindfully in nature. It's the feeling of being so in the "zone" that you are completely one with the moment. Many musicians experience this when they are playing their instruments. The important thing is to have some regular mindful disciplines in place, a repertoire so to speak, so that mood is regulated and you are better able to "just notice" what you are feeling and then let it go. Of course, meditation, journaling, and psychotherapy are also great self-care ways to enhance this ability.

For Geri, practicing a regular form of self-care has been extremely difficult. In fact, during our course of treatment, she strongly resisted it because her shame was so big. It's quite a conundrum because one needs to practice appropriate self-soothing in order to manage shame, but when shame is unmanaged, the last thing someone wants to do is self-care. It was when Geri finally allowed some room inside herself, though, by cognitively working through enough of her issues that she could, in her words, "accept the gift of unconditional love and God's grace."

Even though Geri was not in an emotional place to allow herself the regular practice of yoga at the time we were working together, today she is enjoying yoga and is beginning to recognize its benefits.

---

14   "I believe some of yoga's most profound effects on health have to do with its ability to alter long-standing dysfunctional behavior. People often have unhealthy habits of thought and deed that undermine their health—habits they may recognize but haven›t been able to change.... The modern understanding of the brain is that rather than being a static structure (which is what I was taught in medical school), this organ is constantly remodeling itself, a phenomenon scientists call neuroplasticity. Repeated thoughts and actions can rewire your brain, and the more you do something, the stronger those new neural networks become." Dr. Timothy McCall, (2007) *Yoga As Medicine.* Bantam. http://www.yogajournal.com/for_teachers/2016

Seanne is right. Even now it is difficult for me to maintain a regular schedule of anything related to self-care. Yet, because of the literature, and the urging of Gretchen, my current therapist, yoga is the one practice I continue to return to. When I am mindful of its benefits which I admit, is intermittently, I return to the practice for its centering and calming effects, not the least, the physical needs I have to remain pain-free and active.

Geri Henderson & Seanne Emerton

22

Believer

It is no surprise that I've been conflicted about formal religion. Perhaps the surprise is that I am less conflicted now than I have been in the past. I want to be clear that I am not conflicted about my faith in God and my reliance on Him to heal and support me through my many years of struggle. Perhaps, my faith journey will help those who have had serious questions about God or his love and care.

I attend church regularly. I am a believer. But the details of what I believe fluctuate. The most important element—an omniscient, omnipresent God, whose Son, Jesus Christ, came to earth and whose death is redemptive for all mankind—is the solid basis of my faith. Everything else (theological dogma and detail) does not matter to me very much. I read avidly and find myself looking for answers to the questions of detail among the writings of theologians from varying points of view. I look askance at anyone who claims to "know" anything with complete certitude and am more accepting of writers who engage their audience in mutual exploration of the God-human connection.

In my young adult life, belief in God and His presence in human interactions was not a given. I made several attempts at being a good churchgoer, but the church's teachings were almost impossible to reconcile with my father's behavior. I knew that Jesus had said, "Suffer the little children to come unto to me and forbid them not for of such is the kingdom of heaven" (Mark 10:14), but I certainly never felt that Jesus was protecting me. It all seemed like a huge lie. On the other hand, the teachings of the church had been such an important part of my childhood, the position of God, Christ, and the Holy Spirit so integral to a good Christian life, that I could not easily walk away without guilt. It seemed that my life would never be truly fulfilled without including God. So, I kept wrestling with these issues.

I was caught in this spiritual conundrum for many years until I came to the realization that, above all, God honors our free will. Ergo, we are allowed, on a daily basis, to hurt one another in big and small ways. My yardstick for determining God's willingness to intervene has always been global tragedies like Nazi Germany. God did not intervene then, nor has He intervened in the many disasters and genocides before or since, so I certainly could not expect Him to intervene for me. God does not shut my mouth when I am about to say something unkind, and He does not intervene when adults choose to hurt children. There are times when someone is prevented from hurting someone else and one might say that God was providing protection, but abuse, murder, genocide, and torture are sad facts of life for thousands of people every day.

> So, what is God's place in the mess we humans have made?
> Where is He in my life?

The older I have become, the more I sense a need in myself to know that a God of love is present in my life and that there is something else "on the other side" of the life I am living now. Ultimately, He is my place of reason when nothing else makes sense. Yet, while I find myself consistently depending on His presence, I feel that I hold God at arm's length sometimes. Sometimes, too, the idea of closeness with God has been frightening. One of my bottom line beliefs is this: If I understood everything about how and why God works, He'd be a very small God, indeed.

I find the tension that Geri holds on this internal conflict of who, what, and where God is, admirable and healthy. I respect in her that she asks the questions and lives with the struggle that creates. It has obviously been a lifelong battle. Being brought up in a conservative Christian home steeped in religious doctrine, experiencing sexual abuse from a minister father, living in many countries amongst various world religions, and studying religion in higher education, who wouldn't get confused? Geri's ambivalence, internal conflicting thoughts, and confusion were frequently a therapeutic block. I often felt ill-equipped to address her concerns from a theological standpoint even though I was a religion major in my undergraduate studies. Fortunately, Geri found spiritual support and guidance from her local pastor. Many times I was very grateful for his well-balanced, wise, and kind counsel. I thought of him as a co-therapist. He appreciates complexity in situations and has high empathy, characteristics that were very helpful as he ministered to Geri.

Neither Geri nor I ignored the value of spiritual life in therapy. Naturally, I have to meet the client where she is with spirituality, but I cannot make it her agenda. Some clients do not value a spiritual life. When the client values incorporating spiritual life in the treatment plan, I honor their spiritual path, which may not necessarily be the same as mine.

23

A Crack in the Armor

One day, when I was about 25 or so, I went to the ophthalmologist for a checkup. Before returning to work, I stopped at my apartment for lunch. With blurry eyes, I picked up my mail and climbed the stairs. When I glanced at the mail, I was shocked: my father had sent one of the two letters he ever wrote to me. I imagined all sorts of things were wrong, especially that there was an emergency of some sort, so I took the letter back to work in the church office where I spent part of my work day. The only person there was the main pastor. I asked him if he could tell me what the letter said since I couldn't see. It was quite lengthy, but the only line I remember is this: "I'm sorry for anything I have done that might have affected your decision about getting married."

I've always wondered what precipitated her father sending the letter at that time. Of course, Geri did not ask him directly. Instead, she eventually told him that "...everything will be fine." (Hardly!)

Her father chose interesting words, "I'm sorry for anything I have done..." Well, I guess so! I wouldn't categorize this as a real apology, yet it was something. It shows he may have felt some remorse and had some awareness his actions had indeed negatively impacted her with long term consequences. Little did he know how much!

Even now, I can remember suddenly going cold, looking down. Then, quickly recovering, looking up, and giving him the bravest smile I could. The pastor was staring at me. I quickly said something like, "Oh, I can't imagine what that would have been!" He finished reading the letter, but nothing else soaked in. I left the office as fast as I could and tried to put the whole thing out of my mind.

This was the first time, since the conversation with my mother at college graduation, seven years earlier, where she had vaguely alluded to my father's behavior, that I had been forced to think about the events of my childhood. As a matter of fact, I remember that in college I told people over and over that I'd had a wonderful childhood with parents who were so good I'd want them to raise my own children! Really? I can even remember saying that to my mother more than once, too. What kind of denial was this?

Geri's declaration of a wonderful childhood speaks well to the effort she gave to compartmentalize her growing up years. For the sake of self-preservation (or so she thought) she denied and even recreated childhood memories so much so that her pseudo memories became "wonderful" instead of traumatic. In addition to being the exact conditions in which personality disorders are born, the problem with containing parts of self and one's history to this extreme is that it can easily come crashing down with a single incident.

After my father's letter, any kind of a cohesive life I'd tried to build for myself began to unravel, and I didn't even know why. I was not consciously thinking about my relationship with my father. In fact, I was using a great deal of energy actively trying to forget it. What I was doing wasn't working, and managing my life became increasingly difficult. I stayed very busy working three jobs and beginning graduate school, but as time went on I became ever more depressed and suicidal.

Yes, Geri identified it exactly here. She used a tremendous amount of frenzied energy in a desperate attempt to "forget" the abusive relationship with her father. She ran from herself. It caught up with her, as it does with everyone, and it showed in depressive symptoms that lead to her suicidal ideation.

So, she had no ground on which to stand when the reality of her false self, which had been built from her efforts to compartmentalize, came crash-

ing down with the arrival of this letter. Her center was lost, precisely because it had been false.

I have often said that had I known how long, how dark, and how painful the hole would be into which I fell, I would have tried to stop my fall somehow. I wonder if I could have. Would it have been possible? The fall was rapid and seemed endless at times. The wounds that opened on the way down seemed to bleed and ooze with infection for many years.

It took Geri a very long time to relax into the knowing that she can manage her dark holes. I was unsuccessful in telling her that; she had to experience it. After her move abroad, she would often report feeling anxious about any "down feelings" for fear they would lead to another dark hole. However, with time and care from her good friends and the excellent therapist Geri found after she moved, she eventually became convinced that she could trust others to help her manage. She had indeed begun to build a solid sense of self that would help her avoid stumbling blindly into the dark holes. This book is really the story of Geri building that solid, true sense of self into the survivor she is.

24

"An Angel Held Your Heart"

I was reminded recently of the importance of friends. Actually, I'm reminded of my friends almost every day. It's impossible to say where I would be without them. They have enriched my life immensely and, the truth is, they have saved my life.

The chapter, "Shame," relates that one of the first things I learned when I started therapy originally was that I should find a few friends and try to trust them with the truth. But, fear—the fear that if my friends knew about my past they would not want me teaching their children, let alone want me for a friend anymore—prevented me from being open with them right away. Yet, it was one of the first "homework" assignments of my therapy. I'm sure my first disclosures were timid, panicked little bits of information that left more questions than they answered. What amazed me was how very accepting and loving my friends were. They were amazingly supportive, and my disclosures seemed to deepen our relationships rather than break them. They stayed up with me when I couldn't sleep. They listened, they comforted, and at times, cried with me. Only once did one of them mention leaving me, and that was well into my many years of therapy.

It was a very new and different experience for Geri to talk openly and honestly with anyone about her abusive childhood, let alone friends. Of course, she had to talk to therapists during and post hospitalization. It's one thing, though, to talk to a therapist and quite another to be open and hon-

est about past issues with friends. The fear of rejection was huge for Geri. This was fed by her shame and complicated by the fact that she desperately needed her friends. So, the risk in sharing was compounded for her. She was just in the formative stages of growing her solid sense of self and the foundation was not yet in place. Thank God her friends truly loved and cared for her. They stepped up to the plate full-heartedly, with tender-loving skill and care. The power of this experience can't be overstated. It was primarily this group of friends who provided the impetus for Geri's healing journey. These steadfast, strong, and supportive women weren't afraid to walk along side Geri in her raw pain. They literally held her. No amount of therapy could have done for Geri what these incredible friends did. It was also a gift that her core group of friends, to whom she originally disclosed her past abuse, happen to be emotionally healthy and stable individuals themselves.

The next fear I had was that they'd get worn out—that I was leaning on them so much that they would lose patience and walk away. I tried to be aware of possibly tiring them, but I realize now that I couldn't have been fully aware. There were other times when I made huge assumptions about what they were thinking, why they had said or done things, whether or not they wanted to see me, and so on. I don't know how many times I approached a friend's house and left without knocking. Sometimes, I would drive by to see if their lights were on and then, decide that walking up to the door was too frightening, or it was too late, or any other excuse for not stopping. But later, I would have to call someone out of desperation for contact with a real voice, not my inner dialogue.

I didn't seem to be able to trust my friends or my ability to keep good friends around. Again, I was always surprised by the wonderful people who made me feel welcome and even seemed to want to be around me. Most of the time I did not, and still do not, believe my good fortune. I have been lucky enough to have some of the most wonderful people as friends. Often, we came together over our mutual care of their children when I was their piano teacher. They're intelligent people who were also sensitive and kind and welcomed me among their families and into their homes.

I alluded to one friend who walked away from me for a time. The difference in this friendship was that she was amazingly perceptive and intuitive, and she seemed to be able to push me beyond the place where my last therapy session had ended. What she provoked was more dialogue and a greater need to process what she was asking. In the end, she couldn't deal with what she'd created. It was too much for her, and when I asked her if she needed a break, she said yes. The sense of rejection that event elicited lasted many painful years. It was as if she had pushed me into deep water and then walked away yelling, "Save yourself," over her shoulder. We have both grown a great deal in the years since. We are more transparent and more aware of each other's emotional place than we were before and perhaps even closer.

Geri invests herself fully in her friendships. The ability to have and honor healthy boundaries however, was an issue for Geri for many years. There was a time when Geri would ignore her own needs but do anything to meet the needs of her friends or family. While there is still some tendency toward this, her healing journey has progressed and so has her ability to keep good boundaries. With her growth, her assertiveness has also grown. Though old behavior may have been more indirect and manipulative in an attempt to meet her needs (which came off as "needy"), now she is able to directly (yet politely) ask for what she needs. There have even been times when she has made the decision to end a friendship that seemed to be less than healthy.

Recently, I was asked for my professional opinion on a set of poems by an Arab-American friend, Samr. They were addressed to his wife, and I found them rather erotic and difficult for me to read objectively. I knew he would be disappointed, but I finally had to let him know that I was having a hard time reading his work and responding appropriately. I had to satisfy Samr's insistent need to know why by telling him that notions of romance and love were hard for me because of an incestuous childhood. He became very upset. He is a very sensitive and intuitive man so I was not surprised when he told me later that he'd since experienced a disturbing vision of one of my father's nocturnal visits. He tried to look away, but the vision followed his eyes. Samr said that when he looked more closely he saw that an angel was guarding my heart. Samr believes it means that my core essence was safely guarded during those growing-up years. I'm not so sure it's true, but it is a lovely image that I like thinking about.

Today, I have more than enough friends—more deep friendships and more honest friendships than I could ever have hoped for. Sometimes, I think that I am blessed beyond measure by good friends I don't even see very often. But the Internet keeps me well connected and allows me to stay involved in the lives of many of my friends. When the opportunity arises to get together again, we can easily pick up where we left off.

These days Geri's friendships cover the globe. She is a connector and loves linking up the friends in her repertoire to help others as needed. While she is the first to step in and help when needed, she is also taking better care of herself. This has been a huge achievement and contributing factor to her current mental health. It's symbolic of her health that she can now even entertain the thought that she is worthy of an angel guarding her heart.

She can sniff out someone with an abuse history faster than anything and knows how to intervene skillfully. She is now able to discern the difference between healthy and dysfunctional relationships and has developed the emotional intelligence to hone and nurture the healthy ones, while appropriately setting boundaries in dysfunctional relationships. This is no small feat. The high value she has placed on healthy relationships prevents Geri from taking them for granted. The intense accountability she holds in her relationships brings a deep richness to those fortunate enough to be in her global circle of friends. Geri gains a great deal of emotional satisfaction from these very strong, healthy relationships. This would not have been possible had she not persevered in doing her very hard personal work. It is a lifetime of practicing emotional self-awareness and management skills. It is for all of us, really, but especially for someone with a trauma history like Geri's.

At the beginning of therapy, when Geri displayed symptoms of borderline personality disorder and an intense fear of abandonment, it must have been highly challenging for her friends to hang in there with her. It speaks well for the dedication of these friends who have loyally stayed by her side. They seemed to see that she was more than her symptoms. Maybe they sensed that angel guarding her heart.

25

Diagnosis: BPD

I will never forget the day I walked into therapy and was given the DSM to read.[15]

Well, it wasn't exactly like that! I worked into the topic and then showed her the definition.

At the top of the page were the words, "Borderline Personality Disorder." There were about ten or more indications listed. Seanne said, "Tell me how many of these you recognize." I said, "Seven, maybe eight." She went on to explain what that meant and why it might be important for me to know and understand. Along with that description, I also later found information online. I learned that BPD often results in multiple hospital stays, requires long years of talk therapy, and generally results in a low success rate of recovery. I remember being on an emotional roller coaster for a couple of weeks after learning all of this. There were times when I felt glad to know that some of the crazy feelings and weird responses I was experiencing were not entirely my fault. (I learned that sexual abuse often gives rise to such feelings and responses.) At other times, I felt truly hopeless. Over time, I'd gotten used to living in a head that was difficult to understand, that made me feel crazy most of the time, and that made me

---

15 *Diagnostic and Statistical Manual of Mental Disorder 3, 1990.* American Psychological Association.

think that I had no friends at all some days and didn't deserve them anyway. I had worked hard trying to get better and now had discovered that it might be impossible after all. Was this all I had to look forward to? Just more therapy, more weird relationships, more craziness, and less hope? That was hard to accept.

We had been in a stuck phase of therapy prior to this session, and while I believe I could have managed the session more skillfully by being more thorough in processing the definition of BPD with Geri, I do believe the timing was good to be honest with her regarding this personality disorder. (I had sought peer supervision regarding this intervention prior to the session and was validated in proceeding with it.) We had worked hard together to build trust in the therapeutic relationship. She knew she seemed stalled in "getting better." I also knew it, and we needed to name it. To have avoided truthtelling at this stage would have undermined trust in the therapeutic process. We could no longer dance around it, and she was more ready for the naming of it than not. I felt she needed to understand how her BPD symptoms led to behaviors which appeared to be manipulative out of her desperate fear of abandonment. For instance, she had great difficulty being direct with people. She did not speak assertively regarding her needs, feelings, or desires. Then, she felt rejected when people didn't respond or understand. Her inability to be totally open with me in therapy made progress very difficult.

Eventually—it took a few weeks—I was able to renew my commitment to getting better any way I could. I know that discouragement was not Seanne's intention.

I knew it was a risk, but I trusted Geri not to become suicidal from the knowledge of BPD. It was hard for her to live through the dark, hopeless/helpless feelings it first created, but I had to trust the process. Part of the process is often the client despairing in the recognition of a reality that they want to deny. In fact, the knowing eventually shifted Geri and our therapy process into a new stage of hope and "fighting back." It is a grief process where clients experience loss and what they wanted to believe about themselves. Thankfully, Geri had the resilience, tenacity, and the support system to work through this process. She not only came to a place of acceptance, but she came out fighting. She had obviously adopted the attitude of "This isn't going to define me!"

More often than not, Seanne would remind me of my progress and even I had to admit I was aware of progress in some areas. I came to see that I was not really going around in circles. Rather, it was more like a spiral that slowly rose. I might think I was meeting the same difficulties, but my perspective would be different each time as I rose higher and looked further down on them. I also gained some gradual speed as I learned how to manage the triggers that would precipitate an episode of depression.

The shift I eventually experienced came from two beliefs. First, I have always said that if I understand why I behave as I do, I can work at changing it. Second, I read in many personal narratives that patients suffering from BPD had multiple hospital stays and such difficulty in relationships that they often lost their friends. I was determined to work hard to avoid losing my friends.

The world of diagnosing is always tricky for me. It's part of my job; it's how I get (or don't get) paid by insurance. It can also be an effective tool for establishing the treatment plan with evidence-based interventions, and that is important. Yet, attaching a diagnosis can create a very limiting worldview for both the client and the therapist. If I believe the client is hopelessly destined to be defined by the cluster of symptoms a specific diagnosis holds (and by definition many personality disorders are considered inherent to the personality and therefore chronic), then I cannot guide the client to wellness.[16]

So, I needed to hold the tension of a working diagnosis (and Geri had several) for purposes of treatment but not lose hope myself nor cause her to lose all hope. Many factors influence clients' ability to heal, including their readiness and willingness to engage in change and their ability to feel hopeful. However, clients often have secondary gain to hold onto symptoms (i.e. to gain attention or to reinforce a victim, "poor me" mentality). And some hold onto their diagnosis like a badge of honor. Geri could have very easily worn a "BPD badge" on her shirt and played the role of helpless victim, but she was done. She was ready for a change.

All the work in the world fighting the symptoms of BPD never seemed to eliminate the depression that was always just around the corner. For many years, each recurrence felt like it would never end. These episodes

---

16 _The diagnostic manual was designed as a tool for professionals to communicate with one another, to simplify language describing the cluster of symptoms they were seeing in the client. The purpose is to document the assessed symptoms in the client record so the next clinician who may need to see the client can understand the course of treatment. Obviously, there is no black and white blood test you can do with a client to verify a diagnosis. So, sharing a diagnosis with a client needs to be done thoughtfully and carefully._

arrived frequently, and it was puzzling to figure out when they would leave. I used to think, to say, "I'll never be happy again, never!" But just in the last four years I've realized that my personal history is one of return to a non-depressive state, each time more quickly. Depression does end; the long, dark tunnel is shorter than it used to be. Even during the darkest of tunnels, I seem to be able to remember this most of the time. Depression is not as frightening as it used to be.

Another thing I came to realize was that the things in my head—the assumptions I was making about what my friends and family were thinking—were rarely correct. Once I came to understand that it was my own head playing tricks on me (instead of other people), I was able to learn ways to "talk back" to the old voices, mostly from Father, that had come to live in my head and put me and every situation in the worst possible light. I can now see that people really are glad to see me when they say they are, and I now know that when people ask me to call or stop by they usually really mean it. What a long time it took me to give people the chance to relate to me honestly, and what a longer time it took me to honor them by doing the same!

Yes, Geri implemented cognitive behavioral techniques quite readily once she decided to. It helped that her friends would remind her to "talk back" to her irrational thinking as they would help remind her of "the truth." This was great reinforcement for what I was trying to do with her in therapy. In addition to using cognitive behavioral therapy, I like to incorporate lots of different styles in therapy, all originating from meeting clients where they are. These methods use variations on the narrative/conversational therapy model, which incorporates the clients' language to weave interventions. It involves entering their "world view" (including spiritual, emotional, intellectual, and physical components), listening very carefully, pacing, and mindfully using their language to help them be more consciously aware of their thinking/feeling/behaving process. The ultimate goal is to help the client observe their own processing without judgment, then let go what no longer serves them. This is the art of doing therapy. The art is also in engaging clients by entering but not becoming part of their world with often subtle intervention so that they may even wonder how it is they "got there." I find this way of working sets up the least resistance in clients even though there are times I push when clients want to stall.

The narrative approach that Seanne used with me was an approach I had not previously experienced. It worked well for me because it gave me the feeling that Seanne, having really listened, would know what to do to help me. When other therapists had taken "short cuts" and attempted work in behavior modification, for example, I thought they couldn't possibly understand why my behavior was strange or how to help me change it. It felt as though some therapists worked from a formula and that the exact details of my individual story were unimportant. The details were, however, important to me, and I trusted the person who would listen.

Because of Geri's steadfast dedication to heal and because she chose to do hard, scary work, she was able to lessen the intensity of the depressive and post-traumatic stress disorder symptoms and the borderline personality disorder symptoms. In fact, today she doesn't meet the criteria for BPD or PTSD. The depressive symptoms, however, are stubborn companions.

Geri Henderson & Seanne Emerton

26

Therapists

Finding Seanne took a long time. Once I did and she had accepted me as a client, I was desperately afraid she'd fire me. Even though Seanne was very good at switching tactics, I sensed that some of the things she wanted and tried to do were impossible. I got the sense that we were going the long way 'round to reach goals that she might have managed to accomplish much earlier with others. Each time we hit a roadblock, I worried that she would run out of patience and terminate our work. I also worried that in our small town I had run out of options. After the previous experiences I'd had with therapists, I refused to see just anyone.

I had no idea that she was afraid I would fire her. I was actually concerned she would fire me and abort therapy in the midst of some very hard work we had to do.

First, there was Mark, the therapist who'd threatened me with institutionalization. I learned that therapists had the law on their side and if they decided that I was non-compliant, they could probably present a strong case to the state board about my inability to live on my own.

Therapists are required by law to assess if their client is a danger to self or others. If there is true danger, therapists can, at times, convince the client to voluntarily commit themselves. If the client is resistant or if there is no available family member to assist, the therapist calls law enforcement.

In the state of Nebraska, the process is not unlike other states in that law enforcement assesses the factors determining the need for implementing an Emergency Protection Custody order.

I feared that the more I might protest, the greater would be their proof that I was, indeed, certifiably nuts. I felt that compliance was my one defense. That sounds a bit silly now. How can compliance be a defense? Shouldn't I be learning how to stand up for myself? But at the time, I believed what Mark told me and, despite never feeling any better, continued to show up faithfully every week. Now, I know that his threats had more to do with his own need for income than with my need to see him. Unfortunately, those threats colored the attitudes and thoughts I took with me to every therapist thereafter. Often, I felt as though I was caught in a no-win situation.

In addition to his threats and manipulation, Mark's agenda was unclear. He would tell me about his own life and, I would realize that his childhood was worse than mine. Perhaps, I thought, that gave him authority where dysfunctional families were concerned, but looking back on it, I realize that he had not been able to deal with his own junk and probably never will. He also had a weird way of suggesting I needed sex therapy, and he kept checking with me to see if I was ready. I'm not even sure what he meant. Was he suggesting I meet someone in a hotel? I was vulnerable, needy, and easily convinced I had to do whatever it took to stay out of the institution—a fate worse than suicide. But on this issue, he never won.

This therapist was a disgrace to the profession and, as previously said, had his license appropriately removed. His behavior was unethical and abusive. It is tragic that Geri had to layer this kind of trauma from "treatment" on an already heavy load of trauma.

The other thing Mark did that had a reverse impact on me was to administer an IQ test. I didn't know what it was because he was very casual about it. When he showed me the results, something above 140, he tried to tell me that it indicated high intelligence. The effect of this was to push me further into self-disgust. Why was someone who was supposed to be so "intelligent" so messed up mentally? Surely an intelligent person could figure issues out on her own. And, if my intelligence was so high, why hadn't I done anything useful with my life and for people? Cure cancer? The common cold? World peace? Forget it! All I could do was survive. Clearly, the test was wrong.

During all the time I saw Mark, I had been on medications to handle recurring depression. Despite his failings, he did save my life that first time, and there are things he told me I'll never forget—like the advice that I should tell my friends, or the time he told me that I was running from tigers. When I asked, "What tigers?" He replied, "You haven't seen them because your running has been successful so far." Yes, I was running—as fast as I could, and eventually, faster than I could.

In the end, I had to find a lawyer who would represent me in an insurance fraud case against Mark. He had double-billed my insurance company for months. Because of this and a number of ethical issues brought against him by other clients, he lost his license to practice. After Mark, I went several years without a therapist—until I quit taking meds. I didn't need them, I decided. I was managing pretty well. Of course, I hit the wall once again.

My doctor suggested I see Pamela, a respected psychologist in our town. Almost immediately, I was hospitalized. Another MMPI (Minnesota Multiphasic Personality Inventory), another time spent trying to convince everyone I was well enough to leave. I was still working with Pamela the third time I was hospitalized. This time, my stay was shorter even though I threw the whole folder containing the MMPI against the wall of the hospital room. I'm sure Pamela was shocked, but this test was one of the most annoying instruments I was to experience in all my years of therapy.

I think this is when Pamela suggested the Menninger Clinic, then in Topeka. She explained to me that I would be under psychiatric care for many years into the future but that at the clinic I would be much better in six weeks. As I prepared to leave for Topeka, the clinic began to send questionnaires, including one that went to my parents. I was immediately worried and suspicious. As part of the program, my parents would be required to come to Topeka for a time. I prayed they wouldn't be able to, but my mother said she would. Thankfully, my father said he couldn't.

I explained to my students I would be gone for a while and would probably be writing. This was not a lie. I planned to work on my Master's in Music thesis, a project that had already gone on far too long, as noted earlier. One of my young students, assuming I'd be writing music, said, "Oh! Will you be writing Looney Tunes?" When her mother, a close friend, heard that, she was appalled and worried that I would take it personally. I laughed and said, "No, I don't think so." In the end, probably because of my father's absence and because of my inability to work out questions of insurance, I did not end up going.

After a time of continued work with Pamela and of being medicated once more, I realized that I was running out of answers when she asked me how my week had gone and what I wanted to talk about. At times, I could hardly remember why I was even there. It all seemed so unimportant, and I seemed to be going nowhere. On one hand, I wasn't suicidal, but on the other I wasn't anything! So, I took another long break, managing again as best as I could.

Fortunately, there were activities that I undertook, happy events that occurred and necessities placed upon me that kept me focused in generally positive—or at least not depressive—directions. Some of these I took upon myself; others just came my way.

At some point during my break from therapy, I briefly entertained the suggestion that I should seek out a survivor's group. I have heard that group therapy is a great help for some people. It was not for me, however. I could hardly make myself walk in the room, and, when everyone turned to see me, I wanted to fall through the floor. I made myself go twice but never spoke. The horrific stories I heard there will remain in my memory always, and I haven't been able get the dreadful suffering of those women out of my mind.

Then, perhaps the most important "supportive" event happened: a baby girl was born among my brother's five children. My niece and I bonded almost instantly, and the idea that I could commit suicide became impossible to contemplate very seriously.

During this time, I knew that there were lots of things that didn't feel right, that I really wasn't managing my life very well. But the busyness and heavy responsibility I had for my family was completely absorbing, physically and mentally. Church attendance, which had slipped to nearly nothing, was important again with children to teach and train. At this time, too, I was finally finishing my Master of Music degree.

No, there were too many things to distract me from my depression and struggles and to keep me going. Eventually, however, my house of cards came crashing down once more.

I realized that the church we were attending was not meeting the needs of the children or even my own needs. I was uninvolved and only went because of the children. So, I quit going. Around this time, I became acquainted with several families from an evangelical church close by. I always tried to make time to attend the activities of my students so I found myself there many times for their baptisms, solos, and so on. One of my friends began to wonder if I needed to see a Christian therapist. Maybe that was the missing piece?

From a Christian radio program, I was given a reference for a local therapist, Calvin. My friend went with me to make sure I wouldn't chicken out.

I remember being so afraid of another male therapist and was concerned about what a "Christian" counselor might think about my father—rightly so. First, Calvin made an assumption that when my father had sex with me, I had been tainted by evil. It was not an intentional association with evil, of course, but Calvin believed that the evil had to be exorcised nonetheless. Second, he wanted me to visualize a night scene with my father that included Jesus. Calvin said he was using "theophostic" techniques but, whatever they were, I was terrified.

I had a difficult time embracing the idea of exorcism despite my tendency to be compliant. I went to the minister of my church to ask about this, and he said a godly woman couldn't possibly be possessed by demons. I was grateful to him and quickly dismissed the idea. As for imagining Christ in the midst of my traumatic situations, that was really unhelpful. I felt more shame and embarrassment than I had in a long time. Further, it seemed to me that imagining Christ in scenes of physical and sexual abuse only pointed up, even more, the fact of His presence, watching without protecting. As it was, my humiliation could not have been more complete! That was not a scene I wanted Christ to enter; it was not even a scene I wanted to see, even from this distance. Good grief!

What??? This therapist clearly was not using good judgment, nor perhaps was even trained in treating sexual abuse. "Theophostics" is not an evidence-based, best practice method, but how was Geri to know that?

It should never have been a choice, but had Calvin given Geri the right to choose this method of intervention or not, she could have said that she was not ready for this. It is more likely that she would not have said anything, though, given her passivity.

However, because it was not presented as a choice but rather as a directive, Calvin put Geri in a double bind. She very well could have thought it would make her look like a "bad Christian" if she refused even if she had had the assertiveness to express her hesitancy.

The situation Geri had with Calvin is a good reminder that therapists should be careful to use evidence-based interventions as the primary treat-

ment tool with all presenting problems and that clients should be educated regarding the therapist's training and course of treatment. I doubt Calvin intentionally set out to re-traumatize Geri. Perhaps Geri was a good actor, and he was unable to detect that the outcome of his intervention actually did more harm than good. Regardless, it is tragic that Geri was subjected to this kind of intervention.

Like my experience with Calvin, the redemptive narrative of *The Shack* (a book about a man's spiritual journey and healing of his own sexual and emotional abuse as a child of missionaries) includes a similar scene where God looks on but does not intervene. The book was highly recommended by Christian friends, and I read the first part of it with joy. God is depicted as a big African-American woman, Jesus as a carpenter, and the Holy Spirit as a light and voice in the garden. I could really relate to these images and personalities. They were beings with whom I could connect, perfect in their godliness but personal in relating to humans. It was the culmination of the writer's search for what had really happened to his daughter that gave me a jolt. Mack, the central character of the book, is consoled when he realizes that God never left his daughter's side while she was being murdered and that she was unafraid throughout the experience. That left me really angry and upset at God for his passive presence. Also, a murder scene in which the four-year-old is unafraid seemed to me to be out of bounds of any kind of reality. How could millions of people think this was comforting?

Again, I took a therapy break. Calvin's form of therapy was not the answer. (A great deal of information about the theophostic prayer method is available online, and it is not universally accepted in every Christian denomination.)

Geri just drifted away from therapy, more convinced than ever that she was indeed "bad" and "the problem." Many times, clients just stop showing up for sessions when this kind of thing occurs. They frequently do not have the assertiveness or words to verbalize, especially to an authority figure, when therapy is not helpful, let alone harmful to their current mental state. (We therapists can have quite sophisticated rationalizations for why clients "drop out" of therapy—of course, sometimes blaming the client for not being motivated to change.)

This break from therapy was different from the others in that this time I knew I needed help. Now, I was not only depressed but also running out of hope that I would ever find help. Then, I remembered Seanne, whom I had met through my work in community arts associations and knew that she was a counselor. (Our town is small enough that it is impossible to expect that therapists and possible clients will not know each other.) I began to wonder if she'd agree to take me on. Somehow, it felt right to ask. I was both pleased and terrified when she said yes. What if our work together hit another dead-end before I got well? It could be the end of the road for me.

I was hesitant to take Geri's case for a number of reasons. However, I became easily convinced that she felt I was her last hope. I was most concerned that if I wasn't able to help, her options were very limited in our community, especially at that time. I discussed with her the requirements for such a professional relationship, including strict boundaries. She agreed and was quite respectful in keeping these professional boundaries.

Although the work with Geri was challenging, it was also very rewarding. Her intelligence, humor, and insight made the work highly satisfying. She challenged me in ways that pushed me as a clinician, and I liked that. She was engaged in the therapeutic process and respected it. I looked forward to our sessions, especially after the session with her mother. It was after that session that Geri truly began to accept herself as worthy of healing.

When Geri's new job required her to move abroad, it was hard to say goodbye to her. I did not feel our work was completed (rarely does a therapist really know if the work is complete), and while I celebrated her growth and newfound emotional competency, I was concerned for her welfare when she moved abroad. I knew I needed to continue to keep appropriate boundaries with her (which she had a hard time understanding) and yet do what I could to encourage her to find a new therapist.

This was very difficult for me—to accept, to act on, and to understand. It felt like rejection and still does sometimes. Clearly, we would not be able to do this collaborative work had I not moved beyond it. It felt like rejection and abandonment, and though Seanne and I have discussed it over and over, it still seems hard and harsh, which is antithetical to everything she is. I was very stubborn about finding anyone else, though I did find a wonderful therapist overseas for a while.

This transition was not ideal. While we had reduced the frequency of sessions due to Geri's progress in therapy, I did not consider her ready for discharge. Yet, the opportunity for her to advance herself professionally by moving abroad of course necessitated transitioning our therapeutic relationship. Normally, when clients move, and our therapy work is not complete, I research qualified therapists to whom I refer. With the client's permission, I can communicate with the new therapist, thus paving the way for continued work. That was not possible in this case. Geri was moving to a country where neither she nor I had knowledge of competent therapists. She preferred to wait until she had moved to make personal inquiries for good therapists. So, ethically speaking, I could not abandon her care, yet I could not maintain a traditional therapeutic relationship with her either.

Perhaps it is a good thing that I did not fully understand this end-of-therapy boundary thing. Even now, as I try to think about it, it scares me. My breathing is faster, and I am convinced, whether it's true or not, that I might not have moved away had I understood Seanne's position fully!

In retrospect, I believe I could have better prepared Geri by talking about the transitional process earlier on. However, it was further complicated by the fact that we did not know she would be moving overseas much in advance. Clinically, Geri's ever-present suicidal ideation required an in-person therapist to effectively assess risk. I felt she was even more vulnerable with her move abroad, far away from her extensive support network. I tried to be as available as I could via technology, but it was less than optimal. I did stay in touch with her via email and Skype. I continued to encourage her to find an in-person therapist.

When I arrived overseas, I realized that the cultural differences and challenges would force me to seek help. There were things that happened there that I could not understand and some things that threw me back into fear. On one occasion, I became shocked when the driver assigned to me kept wanting to come to my house. I kept repeating that he *and* his family were welcome for dinner. He ignored this and continued his harassment. At one point, he'd threatened to stop by, and I found myself crawling on the floor of my apartment in the dark that evening to avoid making shadows in front of the windows. Finally, I was introduced to Marilka, a psychologist, another expat, who could work with me in English.

I was elated!!!

Marilka convinced me that this was completely inappropriate of the driver and probably brought on because I was a polite American who smiled. We developed a plan and, with the help of a friend at the university, had phone calls come to me while I was in the car. I avoided eye contact, and eventually the driver was given a new job to do, one that completely removed opportunities for contact with me.

I am grateful Marilka was there for her and empowered her to move forward. Geri learned that indeed she could be okay in the world and has continued to move forward in ways she would never have imagined. It's been hard work, to say the least. She still has to consciously choose to move forward when she wants to hide. But she makes herself do it, and each time she comes out the other end stronger and healthier.

I have come to accept therapy as a necessary and important part of my life. My latest therapist, one recommended by Seanne, has been vital to the ongoing work of writing this book, and I am very grateful to her for wise, intelligent counsel during some difficult times recently. Managing chronic depressive disorder is challenging and requires almost constant vigilance. Her reasoned explanations and challenging questions have helped to continue the process of moving forward. I used to think that complete mental health meant no more medications and no more therapy. I have had to change my mind about this if I want to stay healthy.

Thank God, Geri has found good, competent, and highly skilled therapists to continue helping her on her way. I do not feel the writing of this book would have been possible had she not been under the care of a therapist during the majority of our writing. This has allowed us to keep strict boundaries around what is her therapy and what is the tough stuff of writing. We have been able to manage our relationship as colleagues and friends. It has taken intentional effort on both our parts and has not always been easy. I think it is because we value honesty in the relationship and we have a core trust with one another that we have been able to discuss and work through the issues as they arise. It is a rare and unique kind of relationship. While I am forever grateful we have been able to forge it, I would not recommend this to therapists and former clients. It has been a delicate dance, but somehow we have managed.

I agree that the unique quality of our relationship has allowed us to write together, that it is very tricky, that it is fraught with emotional danger, and that it is probably not wise for most people. When I hear therapists talk or write about the issue of boundaries, I sense a kind of accusation—that clients are asking for or requesting relationships that are inappropriate. I told Seanne that every time we have to talk about this, I feel "icky" and wrong. I have huge issues with rejection that come into play, too, and keep me feeling edgy about this. While writing, we have revisited this a number of times. I am grateful for Seanne's ability to listen without judgment to my fear, anger, and tendency to feel guilty.

I appreciate Geri's candor on the issue as it has helped me more fully empathize with how she has felt blamed for my need to clarify boundaries. Of course, I do not imply it was because she was doing anything wrong. Yet, she easily takes that on. It was my job as her therapist to manage the boundaries, and not every client is as sensitive to boundaries as Geri has been. Today, we are friends, and so my current experience is that managing boundaries is more mutual. We would not have survived had we lacked the communication skills and assertiveness to discuss this slippery slope.

27

Meds

Even though I have had to change my mind about medications, I hate them. I hate needing them. I hate buying them. I hate taking them!

No amount of rational argument about medications has ever convinced me that if I need them, I should take them. It doesn't seem to matter to me that one proponent for medication states that early childhood trauma can alter brain chemical makeup, resulting in the necessity of medication for normal function. Nor does it seem to matter that every time I have stopped taking them, I have spiraled down into a dark hole. Instead, I seem to hang on to the belief that whatever anyone says, my need for medications indicates a kind of failure on some level. "If I were well," I've often said to myself, "I wouldn't need to take pills. The fact that I do is proof I'm not well."

I began my medication trials when I was 17, teaching school on Norfolk Island. I was told that Librium, an earlier anti-anxiety drug (class of benzodiazepine), would help my headaches. I could purchase it over the counter, and so I took it in whatever quantities I thought might help. When I got to college, I told the on-campus clinic that I needed Librium, and they prescribed it.

Really?!

Yes, really.

I was never dependent on the Librium and only took it as needed. It didn't really help my headaches—of course it didn't—but it did make me feel better. One professor's wife gave me the first indication, the first medical assessment of what Librium was when she said, "But Geri! That's what we use on the psych patients in the hospital!" When I graduated, I quit taking the pills and never took anything else until similar medications were prescribed during my first hospitalization.

The first prescribed meds were "old school" and were almost debilitating when I began taking them. I found myself sleeping a great deal and my brain felt foggy. I did not feel as though I would be able to live outside the hospital since I'd lost the ability to stay awake and alert long enough to do more than the most basic personal hygiene. At first, I was so befuddled that I didn't realize that it was the medications that had caused my lack of motivation or direction. Even outside the hospital, when my brain should have grown accustomed to the chemical changes, I was listless, and could hardly remember why I needed to see a therapist.

Eventually, I was able to return to school, though practicing my music and extended periods of concentration were problems for a long time. When I began with the second therapist, she hospitalized me and began new medications.

I have to admit that antidepressants have improved over the years, but my attitude about them hasn't. While my abilities to function and to retain a state of alertness were not as affected with each new med I was placed on, I still didn't take them if I didn't have to (i.e. if I wasn't seeing a therapist that required me to be on them). So, by the time I reached Seanne, I was in dire straits once more.

At Seanne's suggestion, my primary care physician began another prescription, but this time, things like Wellbutrin were available and much less disruptive to my schedule and thought processes. I tolerated the medication much better and so was more willing to stay on them for a while. I continued to make unsuccessful attempts at eliminating them, but I wasn't as resistant as I had been. When I went overseas to teach the first time, I was still on them.

I encouraged Geri to stay on an antidepressant but felt the type needed to be re-evaluated. I encouraged her to see her primary care physician who decided Wellbutrin would be a good choice at that time. She had difficulty taking her medication as prescribed by staying consistent with it. For instance, she would decide on her own she didn't need it or it wasn't helping, so would take herself off and then crash. So, not only did she need a different medication, she also needed to take it as prescribed and to have that evaluated from time to time. Today, thank goodness, there has been a culture shift, and outpatient therapists are in closer communication with our client's primary care physician. Medication is considered best practice and evidence-based for major depressive disorders.

While Geri's abuse history was a core cause for her symptoms and needed to be addressed in counseling, she also had a biochemical need for the medication. Sleep deprivation itself interferes with the chemistry of the brain and adds layers of problems in one's ability to concentrate and function. Therefore, it's an early priority of mine to help clients find ways to get their optimal amount of sleep. I usually explore natural sleep hygiene methods before suggesting they consult with their physician regarding the use of medication or refer them for an assessment to determine the need for a sleep study. It is necessary to thoroughly address sleep issues, or it will be next to impossible to reduce the depressive symptoms. Of course, Geri's sleep problems began early on (as early as the abuse started), so it was a stubborn problem to fix.

Several times, therapists tried to request sleep medications, but I have never liked the groggy feeling I have in the morning and I have avoided them.

While I was working with Marilka, she became very concerned that I needed to have my antidepressant renewed and soon. So, I underwent an assessment by a psychiatrist there, and it was determined that I still needed to be taking something. Now, I had no intelligent way to refuse. As it happened, the college Dean was traveling in the States, so Marilka suggested the meds be sent to the Dean. I balked. I didn't want the Dean to know I needed them. Would she see what kind of medication it was and immediately guess I was a mental case? Would she treat me differently? Marilka's response to my concern was, "Yes, I'm sure she'll get on the school's PA system and announce, 'Dr. Geri needs medications for depression!'" That made me laugh and forced me to admit I was being silly. I asked the Dean. She said, "Sure," and I got my meds. Really, there was nothing to it.

An actual concern at the time was the cost. I did not have American insurance so I had to try to afford them and my therapy out-of-pocket. When I moved to a mission-school in Europe, I was eligible for patient-care programs that provided medications at very low cost or even free. However, I did not seem to need them there. It wasn't until about a year into my most recent move, to the Middle East, that I found myself depressed and suicidal again.

I am taking Citalopram (Celexa) and seem to be getting along fairly well though, as I said before, vigilance and monitoring continue to be important to remaining healthy. At the suggestion of Gretchen and my primary care physician, I have also added a half-dose of Wellbutrin to supplement the primary medication.

Geri finally seems to accept that medication is needed as part of her self-care. This has been hard for her, but she seems to have turned a corner. It is key that she not let her depressive symptoms become unmanaged. As we go to press with this book, Geri is preparing to again move abroad to teach. She is better positioned this time, with lessons well learned.

28

Nebraska and Pauline

Arriving in Nebraska was not planned. Rather, I ended up there because of a bizarre set of circumstances which, in hindsight, might not have been so surprising after all. I had remained in the city of my university after graduation, preparing to take advantage of a scholarship to study in Berlin. In the meantime, I'd rented a charming "mother-in-law" cottage behind one of the city's grand homes. I was working two jobs and taking a graduate course. Within 24 hours, I received a notice that I would have to move and another that I was losing one of my part-time jobs. The scholarship in Berlin turned to ashes with the sudden decline of the dollar in Europe. My friends in Europe warned me not to come. They couldn't find work or even get visas to work, and their scholarships were worth half of what they had been. By this time, I had already turned down the Teaching Assistant-ship in the States I'd been offered. It was too much for me to handle. I just couldn't figure all this out. I called my parents.

They immediately offered to come and help me move to Nebraska where Father was pastoring a small church. Someone they knew, Pauline, offered to hire me on the spot to set up a conservatory of music. As far as my parents were concerned, this was a wonderful opportunity. What good luck after all the bad news and misfortunate I'd recently had! I started commuting from my parents' house to Pauline's business but eventually was convinced to move in with Pauline and her husband to spare me the two-hour commute every day. It seemed like a good idea, especially since it offered the opportunity for me to get out of my parents' house.

Pauline was an intimidating and frightening presence, not only to me but also to her other employees and perhaps even her husband. She was attached to her routine of late arrival at work and late work hours followed by martinis until bedtime. I tried my best to fit in, but it was difficult. I was shy and introverted, and Pauline was completely the opposite. She dressed flamboyantly, exaggerated or lied constantly, and had a temper that was lit by a very short fuse. I never knew whether she was going to be pleased or angry, and sometimes she was both in very short order. I never had more than a moment to myself and became completely dependent on her and her husband for everything, including whatever social interaction I had. I did not meet anyone else for months until I began teaching, and I had very little idea what the town was like. It took me a long time to find my way around.

What was weird was that my bedroom was directly connected to that of Pauline and her husband. If I got up in the night I would either have to go through their bedroom to get to the bathroom or go out to the outside hallway and back into the front door of the apartment. One night I was lying in bed and thought I heard the door open. The next thing I knew, Pauline was crawling in bed with me. She pulled at my pajamas and said, "I'll bet this is something you won't tell your parents!" I remember being absolutely petrified. What on earth was happening? I'm a girl. She's a woman. What could she want? She started fondling me everywhere. My heart sank. So, I thought, here we go again. I will always have someone in my life who thinks they own my body. It was no use pretending to be asleep. She knew I wasn't. These nightly visits were to be repeated over and over.

Yes, this is frequently the tragic pattern until the victim of abuse has done enough work on herself to not have the invisible radar of "abuse me" emanating from her. It was the perfect setup for this perpetrator, complete with the isolation factor and total control of the environment. This was coupled with the fact that the perpetrator knew how desperate Geri was for the job.

Even though Pauline travelled throughout the state on a number of trips, she always made sure that I was with her. I was much more accessible, of course, when we were sharing a hotel room. There were times, too, when she and her husband would quarrel, and I would be used as the go-between. "You tell him that I said..." or "You tell her that I said..." That was painful, too, but worst of all was the feeling that I had nowhere else to go, no one else to talk to, and that my job security depended on keeping her happy.

Of course, once I realized that Pauline was only interested in the conservatory idea as a way to sell more pianos and other instruments, it was pretty easy to figure out that the teaching I took so seriously was interfering with her grandiose plans for herself and the business. On a whim, she would decide I should be at one end of the state or another, and therefore my teaching schedule should be cancelled. After months of stress, migraines, and the emotional extremes Pauline put us all through, I was able to save enough money so that I could move out around the time that a friend from college came to work for her. This gave me the space to see that the parents of the students I was teaching were new friends who had become loyal and supportive. I then quit the position with Pauline. Many nights after that, she would call, drunk, and threaten me with lawsuits because I had stolen her "property" (the students who had followed me when I left). The parents of my students assured me that she could do no such thing, and she eventually gave up and left me alone.

Thank God, Geri had the strength to quit her position and get out of this very dysfunctional system. Her friends supported her and became a lifeline.

My experience with Pauline was horrible and felt like a return to the hell I'd known as a dependent child. But it turned out that this would become a distant memory, condensed in time. In the beginning, I thought that I had somehow ended up in a state I described as the absence of everything: no mountains, no ocean, no cosmopolitan cities, nothing. There was very little cultural life too. When I began commuting to school to return to my graduate work, I discovered that the university campus offered me many of the things I missed culturally: an academic community, fellow musicians, concerts, and other performances. I tried to build a life that would eventually give me some options.

The greatest gift that Nebraska had to offer was the chance to heal among some of the closest friends I've ever had and with the most loyal support group anyone could ever dream of having. Sometimes, I wonder if my real reason for staying in Nebraska such a long time was that I could become comfortable, feel safe, learn to trust, and at last find a path to peace.

Geri Henderson & Seanne Emerton

29

Hunger

Over recent months, I have been attempting to make some lifestyle changes for health. Seanne would say, "You must be ready." I have to agree, I suppose, but most days I feel so unsuccessful that I have wondered whether I really am ready.

I began by asking Seanne how to establish a regular habit of exercise. I'm such a random person that any difficult habit is hard to maintain, no matter how much I seem to know about its importance. Seanne told me that it takes 27 days for a good habit to be established. So, after a couple of false starts, I began sending her a text message abbreviated to say "27-1=26, 27-2=25" and so on through each succeeding day. That worked well, and soon I realized how much better I felt after my body felt stronger and more in shape.

The next thing I wanted to tackle was intentional eating. I knew from previous experience that I have a hard time paying attention to my eating, especially when I am alone. I asked if Seanne would be okay with my food logs at the end of the day. She was very supportive and said, "Of course!" This was a very huge step for me—asking for support and allowing someone to read notes on everything I put in my mouth every day. I didn't want to do it but had read that food logs really help people pay attention to what and how much they're eating. I did that for several weeks and realized that, while it was a way to monitor what I chose to eat and therefore report,

I was struggling to pay attention to the details of how hungry I was, the quantity of what I ate, and the point of satiety.

The next step I took was to try to be very attentive to the food: the portions, hunger, taste, and satisfaction. This appears to have been the moment of truth. There was and has been no way for me to be fully attentive all of the time, but when I first began, I could hardly manage more than three bites without feeling as if I would cry! It made no sense, and I thought, "What on earth is going on? Why is this so hard? Why am I so exhausted at the end of a meal?" I had two choices: Stop eating every time I found I could no longer handle the sadness or the concentration it took (and be hungry in an hour) or shut off my attention so I could finish more of the meal before quitting. I chose one or the other alternative at every meal and still couldn't figure out why I was so sad at mealtimes.

This was good emotional self-awareness on Geri's part. At least, she was recognizing the sadness and trying to generate options to deal with it. This awareness was relatively recent, and she was preparing to move back to the States at the time and therefore was not actively engaged with a therapist. I consciously stayed in the "friend" role with her, but knew she could have benefited from therapeutic intervention.

I did everything I could think of to eliminate distractions without having to deal with my own thoughts. I made a relaxing playlist; I focused on my breathing; I fixed food that was tasty. Nothing was working very well at all. I was still stressed and dissociating for most of every meal.

Parenthetically, I should state that I eat alone most of the time, and so I could think about this three times a day if I wanted to. But, I didn't want to and nearly gave up.

One day, all of a sudden, I remembered mealtimes as a child and even as an early adolescent. We spent most meals together as a family, and they were very stressful! Any trouble I had been in before the meal was brought to the table. The family was subjected to either having my father ignore me, very obviously creating a tense silence throughout the meal, or yelling in frustration about something I was doing or was about to do. I tended to demonstrate my clumsiest behaviors at the table, often spilling things and evoking my father's wrath. I sometimes found myself stuck at the table for several hours after meals trying to manage to swallow something—beets, spinach, okra—that would make me gag. More than once our kitchen helper came to set the table for the next meal, finding me still seated at the table, staring into a plate of something I couldn't eat.

So, I thought, "Maybe this is why I am having such a hard time paying attention." Then, I thought about the time I spend at a meal in the company of others—I am engaged, attentive, and quickly satisfied. I think about and talk about the taste of food, whether or not I like it and enjoy it. That is why it is not possible to dissociate when others are around.

What does this mean? For me, it means that the road to healthy eating is longer and more difficult than I expected. There is much, much more to managing food and healthy eating than a healthy meal. Most of those early weeks, I didn't feel the least bit successful. Instead, I felt crabby or disengaged at meals and inattentive of snacks. I expect that what I am trying to learn is going to be helpful in my quest for physical and mental health.

It is a huge breakthrough for Geri to link her mealtime experiences as a child and adolescent to her eating issues today. Meal times around the family table are a frequent place where power/control issues play out. Her father targeted her, and so a deep negative association was formed. It took Geri a long time to recognize that this seems to be the root cause of her inability to eat mindfully. This is a work in progress, and I feel confident she will achieve success in managing it. Awareness is the key. She feels a sense of mastery when she stays mindful during the quiet solitude of her meals yet can still easily go into shame when she does not stay mindful. The good thing is that she is noticing and is articulating her experience. There is hope!

Most recently, through no apparent further reason, when I returned to the States I had a sense of the correctness of healthier eating. I found out about a program from family members who were happy, healthier, and at goal weight that made a great deal of sense scientifically.[17] I have not had issues with attentiveness, satisfaction, or the need to make an effort to prepare food. While it is a challenge when I am not alone, I find I can quickly return to it as soon as it is possible again. I wish I knew why that is. I don't, but I suspect it has something to do with taking the time to learn how to be attentive. Too, I have discovered that hunger is not all physical. Satisfying emotional hunger needed to come first.

It is marvelous to see Geri truly succeed in the area of respecting and honoring her body. It has taken a long time for her to reach this place, and I agree that it has a lot to do with satisfying emotional hunger. I do not find it coincidental that her weight loss (she currently has lost 25 pounds in a

---

17   Barrett, Pearl P., Serene C. Allison and Monique L. Campbell. 2002. *Trim Healthy Mama.*

healthy and effortless manner) accompanies the claiming of her story and the completion of this book. She is no longer hiding from herself or anyone else. She is living amidst her close family and friends. She is feeling truly loved for who she is. She has let go of some of her shame. Maybe, she was hungry for her Self and has now found her.

30

The Truth about My Father

What is the truth about Papa? People tell me that what he did was heinous, horrible, awful, and even criminal. I think about it and realize that, if it were any other child/person, I would agree, completely. At the moment, I cannot feel much of anything. Gretchen says that being unable to get in touch with some form of outrage and grief about what was done and what was lost to me means that I continue to take on some amount of guilt for what happened. Seanne has asked me, over and over, it seems, what I am afraid of. If I am afraid of something—perhaps some big, long-buried emotion—I certainly do not know it and cannot sense it. I feel stuck, and even though I continue to work on it, I sense a need for some kind of blow to the head to get even close to accepting the truth about Papa.

I've always thought that if I understand the "why" of something, I can work to resolve it. Often, that's true, but this issue feels intractable. When I try to get close to the reality of what happened, I seem to understand, intellectually, what happened but the girl does not seem real to me or, when she does, she is not me or the man is not my father. In other words, making a real connection with the girl, that she was me, and with the man, and that he was my father, seems impossible. I guess the point of writing about this is more of an admission that this is truly hard and especially so when the abuse began before memory and when the beliefs about myself and about my father are so entrenched. It is discouraging to think that I have struggled with this for such a long time and that I keep ending up in this same place at some point in therapy.

My current therapist, Gretchen, has told me that she understands that the abuse was very, very early—that the holes in my memory are there because of intense stress around what was happening. When she asked me if I wanted to remember, I told her no. I still have plenty of material to work on without knowing more detail about what happened. When she asked me to say out loud that my father was a predator, and after that, a rapist, I became so uncomfortable I grabbed the blanket I always carry along to therapy and covered myself up to my eyes. At last, I got to the parking lot and sat in my car, completely undone. I sobbed for a solid hour and became completely numb. These were feelings I thought were behind me. I had no idea that saying the words would open a dam like that.

Gretchen explained that I had broken a long-held family belief and a family taboo. I felt horrible for days! As usual, I believed I would never be happy again. I was sure I wouldn't survive this latest round of misery. I was angry at Gretchen for pushing me into the "deep end," her metaphor. I lashed out at Seanne. Everything in me rebelled and did not want to do this work. Then, I retreated to my usual mental default of blaming the girl.

Gretchen had given me a book to read by Anna G. Salter[18] that I was almost afraid to open, much less read. On the other hand, I soon developed a strange fascination in what she had to say because her interviews with the prison inmates reminded me of someone—my father. It was an eye-opening experience. The more I read, the more I realized that the rationalizations I always use to justify blaming Little Geri are completely wrong. In the face of thinking like this, there is no way the child could ever be at fault. Gretchen explained, as has Seanne, that my thinking was shaped by a child's need to feel safe, to be able to tell herself that she was not living with a monster, that she had to be the one who was wrong. I don't know how long it will take to change my mind.

Was he a monster? I cannot help having a certain amount of sympathy for a man who knew better, whose own childhood issues were so huge that he became the warped, twisted person we knew.

As we have seen, Geri is extremely high in empathy on the EQI scale. She has high empathy (almost too high) for everyone else but herself. This could be better managed if her assertiveness was equally high. However, she struggles with assertiveness, with standing up for herself and speaking her own needs. Her voice was taken from her maybe even before she could speak.

18   (2003). Predators, Pedophiles, Rapists, and Other Sex Offenders. Basic Books: NY.

As a result, she easily puts herself in other's shoes and shows high compassion for them, including her own father. She has seen him more as a victim (and we know he was a victim of his own sexual abuse) and not a perpetrator. She has compassion for the man. This would appear to make forgiveness easy for her. However, it's pseudo-forgiveness because she does not stand up for herself and her own needs; she surrenders her voice and her needs. True forgiveness is possible because of power within. She is still in the process of trying to claim that power. I hope she will master it because forgiveness is first for ourselves, to release us from that something which will eat us alive, that will destroy our joy and our ability to love fully and openly. She is almost there but at this writing not quite.

Her current therapist, Gretchen, is working hard with her to see her father for who he was: a sex offender who robbed her of her full life. Since he is now dead, she has a better chance at fully stepping into the awareness that indeed he was a criminal and would have been in prison had she reported her abuse as a child (and if the system existed on their island to prosecute him). As we have seen, a victim's sense of personal power can be rebuilt, but the wounding is deep and complete repair often impossible.

Geri Henderson & Seanne Emerton

31

Light at the End of the Tunnel

I have a real hesitancy to believe that I can gauge where I am emotionally with more accuracy than in the past. Still, I thought it might be useful to try to explain what the headspace of a 60-something is like after years of therapeutic work and figuring out how to live and how to have faith. I've been able to live a number of years where dealing with one issue or another from the past does not have to be a priority every day. At the same time, I realize that a "Gold Star" is not going to be awarded for having achieved perfection in all areas or having resolved all issues. I also know it is dangerous to think that I will not have to deal with anything troubling again. I understand that were I to continue in intense therapy, the things I could or perhaps should deal with would be never-ending, but I suspect that almost anyone, whatever the past experiences, might say the same. Until recently I, along with the help of wonderful friends, have been able to ride safely over the bumps in the road most of the time.

Again, this is high emotional self-awareness on Geri's part, as well as enhanced reality testing. Both of these EQi (Emotional Quotient-Inventory) traits have grown in her since she began her healing journey. It's new for her to enjoy this deepened sense of self-awareness and reality testing as she more effectively measures her subjective experience against objective reality. This new ground is clearly an outcome of the hard work she has done. She knows everything isn't perfect (when is it, ever, with any of us?), yet she recognizes a newly-found freedom in herself as she has become increasingly symptom free.

When I am not in the midst of it, I know that depression, when it comes, is not the beginning of a scary spiral that will automatically lead all the way to suicide. I realize that taking medication is better than feeling lousy or worse. I understand that I'll probably always resent that. I realize that my inner dialogue is loud and wrong most of the time even though it seems completely true.

The power is in the recognition that her inner voices aren't always reality-based. This, coupled with her core acceptance that depression is a frequent guest in her life, has been huge in her ability to find a sense of peace from all the chaotic upheaval of the abuse. She seems to find her center rather quickly these days, which tells me she is managing the depression and it isn't managing her.

Recently, I had a chance to ride another wave back into the trough of depression. I can look back on it and say it was really no worse than it ever has been. It still felt never-ending and very sad. As I looked into its black depths, it was filled with despair, hopelessness, self-recrimination, and all the other familiar feelings that seem so real. The "truth" of the inner voices was the same believable message, "You've made a mess of things and deserve to feel this way. Anything good you've tried to do has failed, etc., etc." But the wave that seems to push me down also seems to bring me back to the surface, gasping for air, grateful. The energy of waves is both down and up, and knowing how to ride them and having the patience to expect the upsurge is a skill I'm trying to learn.

Another metaphor that I've been repeatedly reminded of is that of an onion with layers that seem to have no end. There is always another issue, yet to be discovered, uncovered. That can be discouraging and ruin my growing self-confidence. I gain some sense of security, and suddenly, for reasons I have to learn or find out later sometimes, I am in emotional trouble yet again. That's no fun, but it's clear to me that certain fears, uncertainties, despair, and frustrations that are deep and old never go away completely. I guess it is unrealistic to expect anything different. Childhood is important for learning about the world, relationships, play, and a whole host of things. When most of a childhood is missing, so are the pieces that make up a complete life. I don't think about it much, though, unless I am forced to try to peel back another layer. And, like an onion, some layers bring tears. There comes a time when it is more important to get well than to keep trying to avoid the pain. Where is the core, the center? I don't expect I'll ever know. When things get completely unmanageable, I go back to therapy.

Living without ever really feeling her "core" is beyond frightening. It can shake her whole foundation because her foundation feels weak to begin with. Yet, I find Geri's ability to accept what it is quite healthy. Because she has high sensitivity and high emotional self-awareness, she is heightened in her sense of loss regarding this issue. When I encouraged her to get more therapy she followed up on the recommendation without much resistance. It is hard for her to accept that therapy seems to be an ongoing part of her life. Yet, I celebrate that her efforts to get well and move forward, rather than avoid the pain, have paid big dividends.

There is a positive message that I always seem to be able to believe and accept now and that is the recognition that I am a good teacher. I have enjoyed some successes in my career and have numerous close, valued connections with former students. I have learned to measure my teaching abilities objectively and see the successes as real and consistent rather than a sudden, good, great fortune that cannot be repeated. I recognize that I can connect well with students and that this has helped establish a rapport in the classroom that creates a positive and safe learning environment.

I am a good friend, sister, and aunt. I can accept that now and rarely doubt it. I remember, though, that I used to be so very insecure about my relationships! I wondered if people were angry with me when I didn't hear from them. I spent a great deal of energy worrying about what I had done, how it might be perceived, and what people were thinking. Part of one's ability to let that go comes with age, I think, but the other part is learning to trust that when people say they love you, they miss you, or they care, they really do mean it. It makes sense now that I have the wonderful friends and relationships I have because my friends are responding to the things they see in me. I can see that they make choices I respect about other friends they have.

Geri's self-regard has dramatically increased as another outcome of her healing journey. She can finally receive love and not just give it. This creates a beautiful ripple effect because the people in her life are then drawn to her even more. There is not a manipulative sense about her because she is more direct and assertive in her communication. She gives/she receives, and she gives a lot. Yet, it is more in balance, thus allowing a healthy complementar-

ity in her relationships. She used to give, give, give, and because she didn't feel worthy, she did not allow herself to receive. There was an unrealistic expectation from her toward others that they should give as much as she did, or it meant, somehow, that she was not valued, cared for, or truly loved.

(Thoughts of equal reciprocation were rarely a part of my thinking. I believed I wasn't worthy of their friendship in the first place. When I was disappointed, there was always a way I could make it my fault, often ending up apologizing for something I perceived I'd done.)

The symptoms of Borderline Personality Disorder (BPD) that disturbed, depressed, and paralyzed me for a time hardly ever bother me anymore. I took an online test just now and scored 19 out of 33 for a "possible" BPD diagnosis. I can see from the questions that I could have easily scored in the "severe" category earlier.[19] My friendships are stable, and I can count on them as surely as they can count on me. I can usually control my thinking so that my thoughts don't run too far away from what my rational mind knows to be true. My mood swings have almost completely subsided. However, when I saw the question about anger—sudden outbursts of anger—I had to admit that yes, that has happened and just recently. I hope I am learning to step back from those sorts of situations and to remember that the person I might be talking to is really not the authority, not the rule-maker.

The fact that BPD symptoms no longer rule her life is an amazing and wonderful outcome for Geri. I say amazing because it usually is very difficult for someone to deal effectively with borderline personality characteristics. The anger she reports seems justified, and I celebrate that she doesn't stuff it as much as she used to! She has grown her assertiveness skills which contributes greatly in helping keep the borderline symptoms at bay. She is rarely aggressive and hardly ever passive these days. True assertiveness requires practice, mindfulness, and intention. I respect that she honors her own integrity to confront situations that do not align with her values. Yet, she confronts in a direct, honest manner, allowing others the respect of directly communicating back.

I have read so much about sleep, some of it required in the course of therapy, so I know that my poor sleeping habits have been a huge factor in my struggle with depression as well as uncontrolled negative thoughts.

---

19   http://psychcentral.com/quizzes/borderline. htm

I can report that I am aware now when I experience exhaustion and make every effort to go to bed when that happens. Even more surprising to me is that my evening routine has increasingly made going to bed and sleep a welcome end to the day. There are many nights I find myself asleep until morning, 6-7 and even 8 hours of sleep at time. I no longer believe that sleep is a waste of perfectly good work time. I recognize that I work better having had restful sleep. Just this week I looked at my bed and thought, if I were sick, truly sick, I could stay here for a few hours. Fortunately, I have hardly ever been stay-in-bed sick any time of my life (except for migraines).

Geri has made remarkable strides in the area of sleep. Her empowerment of self has allowed her to be intentional with sleep, and she has come to value it more than ever before. This helps her practice good sleep hygiene, facilitating deeper and longer which is good sleep practice for managing depressive symptoms.

My general health is pretty good. I do exercise. I never binge or have more than one drink and not that often. The best thing is that my migraines have diminished greatly, and I have better ways of managing them when they do show up. I realize my weight is an issue. I just have not wanted to deal with it, no matter how important I know it is. Anyone who has tried to lose weight knows this very well. If only I could be a body-less head! Recently, I have had some success in weight loss.

Spiritually, I am much more settled with the ambiguities of a human's poor comprehension of what God does and allows. I feel comfortable knowing that God is in control. That does not mean that I have to understand what that looks like or how that affects others. I only have to understand what that means for me. I am secure in my faith and trust in God, and it is uncomplicated by precise theological dogma. I am more concerned that people of faith practice what they believe—that they demonstrate kindness, charity, and concern for the poor and weak of the world.

I am so grateful that Geri has been able to find peace in her spiritual journey. As she has said earlier in this book, a big part of her internal conflict when treatment began was her inability to reconcile a loving God with her abusive experiences. It was a long and slow journey for her to examine and deal with her spiritual questions openly and honestly. It required her finding a member of clergy with whom she felt safe and who not only was well trained to deal with the complexities of her issues but who also embraced these complexities and didn't patronize her with simplistic answers.

Professionally, I have found that the things that most academics value—research and publishing—are things I enjoy but are not things that are as necessary as they once were. I used to be able to lose myself for a whole day in a library, never thinking about physical needs, never needing more than water to keep going. Given the right circumstances, I would be happy to do that again, but I know now that I would not be satisfied with that forever. I have come to realize that for me, rewarding work means work that has human value in leaving things better than they were for people, making a contribution. I don't think this is particularly high-minded, altruistic, idealistic, or unreasonable. I think that anyone who is really in touch with themselves spiritually hopes to be able to look back on a life spent well, doing good, improving the world in some way. Being the best teacher I can be could be enough, I suppose, but somehow it is not. I have too many students for whom attempts to pass my classes are just barriers to graduation. Perhaps this book is one of the ways I can try to help.

Making some kind of sense out of horrible situations and trauma is a vital key to healing. Geri is, by nature, a giving person who wants to make a difference and leave the world a better place. I celebrate her ability to manage her symptoms so that she can truly do this. She has lived in many challenging situations in her professional positions abroad that, even under the best of circumstances, require extra skills to navigate. She has accomplished that and has flourished in her environments. She has been able to invest herself completely in her work and goes above and beyond to take on issues, often in less than receptive environments. Her passion for making the world a better place is indeed high. Her suffering would have been exacerbated by an inability to do what she is called to do.

When I was about 11, I used to fantasize about becoming a nun. Wouldn't that be nice, I used to think, to live in a safe place, surrounded by praying, devoted women? While other girls were reading books about dancers, scientists, nurses, and teachers, I was reading books about nuns. I was fascinated by their lives and commitment. I thought that was something I could do, too. But, obviously, my life has not turned out that way. I have lived outside the presumed safety of the convent, dealing with everyday issues, struggling with the boring and quotidian details that fill everyone's lives. One of those is sexuality. I hate to say it, but it is an important issue for most people and a good thing, too, for most people. I've remained single and celibate.

Another thing I used to think about was what it might be like to have a healthy, intimate, sexual relationship with someone. Would it ever be possible? Now, I don't think about it at all. I enjoy my single life and have close friendships, as well. I don't feel as though I've missed out, either, in not having children of my own or in not having a sexual relationship with someone. As a matter of fact, I have become more and more introverted, enjoying my alone time so much that I cannot imagine being happy sharing it with anyone else on an ongoing basis. I realize I've become more exacting and particular about my habits—the way I do things, the way I like things done—and cannot imagine giving that up to change for anyone. But, I have never been in love, either. Perhaps people in love willingly give up their privacy and fussiness?

Geri's ability to find peace with her sexuality is another hard-won victory. Obviously, this is an area that is difficult for incest survivors to reconcile. Many either become overly promiscuous or shut down sexually. While Geri has experienced this full continuum at times in her life, she has not denied the need to work on this area and, as a result, has come to a place of acceptance and, in fact, satisfaction with being single.

Because I have lived overseas most of my professional life, people use words like "courageous," "adventurous," and so on with reference to the life I lead. I don't see it that way at all. I have gone where positions have taken me, and the longer I have been abroad, the more relevance I have to those positions than I do to positions in the US. I am not averse to moving back to the US, but I need to work and cannot imagine not working. The chances of finding work in the States diminish with each year I have been away.

My family's pain over disclosure and my choice to let go of anonymity for the sake of this book have brought new waves of shame and pain for which I was unprepared. The idea of a completely honest and open book wasstill very fresh when I told Seanne that dealing with this new pain, the pain and fear of my family, was like running barefoot on the beach, oblivious to the broken glass hidden just beneath the surface. It is stupid to run barefoot over broken glass, and it would be better to realize that no matter how much my mind has changed, there will always be broken glass just beneath the surface. I must learn to remember that and protect my feet, metaphorically, by being prepared for the sharp shards that can suddenly cut without warning. Dealing with new wounds always feels like a setback. Sometimes, it even feels as though these wounds are just like the early ones, the ones that felt like they would never heal. I want to believe regression or any other setback shouldn't happen at this stage of my life, but it does. Some wounds heal completely; they really do. For some, I never will develop a thick enough skin to withstand a barefoot run in the sand. And some of the broken glass is too sharp not to cut.

No, the beaches I run on are not completely safe, but my protection is better. I know now my wounds will heal.

I went back into therapy with Gretchen because dealing with the family issues brought up areas of hurt that were too difficult for me to manage alone. I have alluded to the mode Gretchen is using to help me regain my security. What is different this time, besides the therapist, her personality, and methods, is that I am much more aware now of how I am working, and how I am not working. Mostly, I try to work hard, but this stretch of beach feels particularly laden with glass. A full description of this work is not possible here because Gretchen's voice is missing from this section as we are still working together. However, I see progress, and I have hope.

So, what is this "light at the end of the tunnel?" It is the light of survival, but more than that, it is the light of hope and healing, a light that cannot be completely extinguished. I see the light as brighter and steadier with each year. Though it disappears from time to time as the road curves around one obstacle after another, it is always there, closer than before.

Select Publications of MSI Press

A Believer-in-Waiting's First Encounters with God (Mahlou)

A Guide to Bliss (Tubali)

Blest Atheist (Mahlou)

Creative Aging (Vassiliadis and Romer)

Divorced: Survival Techniques for Singles over 40 (Romer)

El Poder do lo Transpersonal (Ustman)

Forget the Goal, the Journey Counts (Stites)

How to Be a Good Mommy When You're Sick (Graves)

Joshuanism (Tosto)

Lessons of Labor: One Woman's Self-Discovery through Birth and Motherhood (Aziz)

Living Well with Chronic Illness (Charnas)

Of God, Rattlesnakes, and Okra (Easterling)

Puertas a la Eternidad (Ustman)

The Marriage Whisperer: Tips to Improve Your Relationship Overnight (Pickett)

The Musings of a Carolina Yankee (Amidon)

The Rose and the Sword (Bach and Hucknall)

The Widower's Guide to a New Life (Romer)

Thoughts without a Title (Henderson)

Understanding the People around You (Filatova)

Widow: A Survival Manual for the First Year (Romer)

CPSIA information can be obtained
at www.ICGtesting.com
Printed in the USA
FSOW03n0734131116
27320FS